At school the teachers would sometimes ask the class what they wanted to do after they left school, some of them would say a fireman, army, doctor, etc but not me I told them I was going to work in the fish. My next door neighbour was Jim Wyness, he offered me a job in Marine fisheries. Off I went two weeks before I officially left school. I remember getting off the bus at Bridge Street and walking down South College street, as I got further down beside the Ferryhill Tavern the smell just hit me, directly across from there was the arches and most of them was occupied by fish merchants. Empty boxes piled up outside, barrels of fish guts, it was an eye opener for me as I had never ventured down there as I was from the other end of the city.

These cavernous railway arches, which form the viaduct carrying the main line south from Aberdeen, were on short term let to a number of small fish – merchants firms. A row broke out when merchants were told to carry out sanitation improvements or move out.

The fish merchants that were in the arches round about that time were Quality Counts, Morrisons Transport, Piper Seafoods, Alistair Ross, Andy Ewen, John Law, Bob Henderson, Pioneer fish Company, Ashley Craig, Ernest Cox, Edward Ladwinies, and Rosangs.

RALMOND RICHARDS
Started work in 1970 in the arches at South College St, you had Richards then Gary Wood. Derek Clark and their mother in law, Jimmy Wood and Bill Sinclair, then we had the box and chemical place, Fred Patterson, Gary Wilson, Davie Dow. There was a lot of 'cummings' and going on at South College street at that time. David Baxter was a manager in Rutherford brothers, then started on his own after that. Rutherford built the Hi Fry cafe on the corner and the fish house under that.

SONNY WALKER
Jim Wood was a nice guy I worked for him when Billy Sinclair was the gaffer. I remember when I was a kid my father took me to Mastrick community centre to see him painting himself in gold to show off his muscles.

JIM WOOD & PETER ROSS
At the dee raft race taking second place in 1979

DOUGLAS McGUIRE

Jim Wood and his brother in law Bill Ewen bought Carnegies fish and that's what started Polarfish. Jim was Mr Scotland he was all muscles but couldn't unload a fish lorry, the boy's used to tell him to get back in the office lol.
You had Stuart Geary, Jack Richards, Vikings Harry Gunn.

One of my favourite fish merchants but I never worked for was Jimmy Wood, he would always stop and talk every time he passed you and he never look down his nose at anyone. Jim is in his nineties now and still going strong playing golf three times a week.

AUDREY McGREGOR

I worked in the arches around 1966 it was the basics back then, we didn't have a bothy we had to sit on fish boxes to have our tea also had to go to the Hi Fri cafe to use their toilet, the guy we worked for was called Alex and was a bit of a chancer as we were always chasing him for our wages on a Friday. The guy borrowed £100 from Martin Richards mum and dad to pay the staff their wages,
he cashed the cheque and legged it out of Aberdeen and never to be seen again. It was the best money they ever spent because they took over the business and went on to have a very successful business for many years.

Everyone in the fish trade knew Freddy Paterson, what I can remember was his firm used to cut some amount of fish in the arches. I went in one day to see him about a labouring job and because he was busy all I got was 'fucking this and fucking that' so I just walked out the door as fast as I could. At lunch times you would always find him in the Ferryhill or the Anchorage. I Got on well with his sons Donald and Alan. I heard he sold his company and moved abroad.

MIKEY MILNE

Worked in the fish most of my life I started in Fred Patersons in South College street and was there for fourteen years, my first job in Freddy's was on the skinning machine then on the finning machine and then learned to be a block filleter.

FRED PATERSON

Ally Thompson also had the arch in between Jim Wood and Freddie Paterson on South College street and that's where the partnership of Couper and Thompson started, back then about 15 years ago it was very common for two or three companies to be sharing the same arch, after that Ally went on to buy premises in Palmerston place.

My very last working days after 16 years in the fish trade was working for Ally and Hilda up at Deep Freeze in Tullos, cutting mackerel on stonage and making very good money but it was a feast or a famine because some days we had tones of it and then we could have went days without any work. It was mostly Hilda that was up there running things and I didn't see much of Ally. Hilda was so nice to all the staff and such a lovely person.

ALLY & HILDA THOMPSON

My first day at Marine it was such an eye opener for me, I was only sixteen and a bit naive and it didn't take much for me to get a red face (beemer), like everywhere else it was always the young ones that got the piss taken out of them. The place was just a small arch and what a shithole it was! You couldn't swing a cat in the toilet and if you were bursting for a pee and someone was in there, you just had to find a corner to piss in. I witnessed a few filleters open up their boiler suites and just have a piss under the filleting table, no health and safety in them days. Opened up in the morning and straight to the bothy to get changed, everyone would pick up their welly boots turn them upside down and give them a good shake I asked why people were doing that with their boots and the reply was that they were just checking to make sure there was no mice inside them. You couldn't leave any food lying there as it would have been all gone by the morning.

CHRISTINE FRASER

I worked in the fish for 26 years for my step dad Freddie Fraser, we had loads of laughs and what you seen was what you got. I put on a pair of wellies one day and started to work away and then felt a lump in my welly boot, when I took off the boot there was a dead mouse inside it, one of the guys thought it would be funny to play a joke on me.

The tax man went into Frafish once and asked the owner Freddie Fraser to see his tax books. Freddie told them that he didn't have them because the mice had chewed them all up, which was true..

There were some characters that worked in Marine, you had Jim Wyness the gaffer, Dod Gray, Denis Barbour, Gordon Wyness, Betty Nerie and a few other filleters, lassie called Una packing the fish, Stuart Cummings dog skinner and labourer, Charlie Farman dog skinner, Davie Leiper driver and me just the 'skiffy'. My first job that morning was to go up a ladder on top of the bothy to clean up all the cardboard boxes that was kept there and as I started to climb the ladder someone shouts "watch where you walk up there as you will fall through the roof" I'm thinking to myself, Cheeky fucker as I was rather big, But they wasn't joking as the roof was rotten and not very safe.

After a couple of hours in walked this little guy who had just came back from the fish market and his name was Alfie Milne. The workers used to call him Rickets behind his back for some reason. He was the manager and for the size of him, he was some grafter but what a moody fucker he was. He didn't really speak to you, he just muttered and most times I couldn't work out what he was saying. God forbid if I ever asked him what he just said, he would just point over to what he wanted me to do and start mumbling fucking this and fucking that. Couple of hours after that, up pulls this big flashy Rolls Royce and in walks this guy with a three piece suit, holding a leather briefcase. He walked straight past me and into the office. Finds out it was our boss Alex Main, electric wires hanging out everywhere, rotten roof, a toilet the size of a telephone box, mice having tea party's at night and this guy walks in looking the part of some big showbiz star. That's when I realised it was true what people said...Fish merchants were loaded and made a fortune in the fish trade.

COLIN EVANS

Back in the days a lot of fish merchants drove about in Rollers or Bentley, Fred Patterson, Thanie Walker, Jocky Greive, Ashley Craig, Joe Little who had a Lamborghini, Herbert Cox had a few Mercedes and Ally Slater had a lot of real vintage cars and even had a vintage yellow Rolls Royce.

ALAN MITCHELL

One of Ally's cars was rented to the film makers of the movie Lawrence of Arabia.

GEORGE LEIPER

In 1967 my dad and uncle George (G & D Leiper) each bought an Armstrong Siddley Saphere and think they were about £1,200 at the time. There were only 6 that came up to Scotland, 3 to Aberdeen, and Charlie Brass had the other one. Posh or what ?

Jim Brander also had a blue Rolls Royce which was owned by the TV magician David Nixen, Dr Francis Clark had a Jensen, Chris Cummings and Davie Dalgliesh had Jags, Jocky Grieve had a roller and it would sit outside his premises all day and his workers would jump in it with their fishy clothes and boots. One guy who worked for him used to drive it up to the brew to sign on. Jocky once paid for all his staff to travel down to Blackpool for the holiday weekend while he drove down in his roller.

Also at that time in Marine they had a young lad called Ally who came in on his school holidays, he stayed up in the farm in Balmedie just a few yards from Alex Mains house. Allys' father Norman worked on the farm and did a lot of work in Alex Mains grounds, after he left school Ally came to work full time, he wanted to be a buyer in the fish market and I'm not joking, I have never seen anyone so passionate about buying fish that's what he always wanted to do. Most times he was taken down to the market to get trained up, but the day's he didn't get to go he was kept in the fish house, Oh my God, I got it the whole day from him as he hated it. Ally went on to work as a buyer for the rest of his life for Marine, but sadly passed away a few years ago at a very young age. I didn't find out until months later and was gutted because Ally was such a nice lad.

R.I.P ALLY DAVIDSON

GEORGE BAXTER

I used to pick Ally up when he just left school at his mums house at Balmedie beside the church to take him to Peterhead market when I worked with Porters.

After a couple of days at Marine I started to enjoy it, I got to know the staff better and started to have a laugh with them all. One guy in particular hat tused to crack me up was Denis Barbour, he had us all in stitches. One of my favourite of his that I witnessed was around about nine o'clock one morning and in walks Denis a couple of hours late, with his dog following behind him. Denis goes up to Alfie the manager and says to him, "Alfie I will have to go home and take the day off as my dog has followed me to work" Alfie said "OK then I will see you tomorrow" I looked over and seen a few of the filleters silently laughing away to themselves. I asked one of them what was so funny they said " he hasn't got a fucking dog." Next morning Denis came in and told us the story... he couldn't be arsed working that day and he had already used about every excuse in the book for not going into work, so that day as he left his house he grabbed a few sausages and the first stray dog he came across he gave it a sausage and enticed the dog with the other sausages so it would follow him to work. The great thing about the fish trade was every fish house had a Denis Barbour in it.

AUDREY McGREGOR

Worked with some characters over the years, Always something or someone to make us laugh, worked with some arseholes as well though. I loved Stanley Robertson he always had a traveller's tale to tell us, he told me one day that he made up most of his stories but he was so funny and a true gentleman.

ARLEEN McDONALD
You had Tucker Donald the singer, it was more like a karaoke line than a production line, we would all join in with him and sing like we was on the voice or something. When I was just a wee lassie working in Alex Ross I was told to get egg white to dip the fish in it to make it shinie !!! Ffs gullible eh!! My father Frankie Raeburn was a caricature, one Friday when he was working in Eddie & Forsyth he cut his thumb and went over to Taylors shop on Victoria road and bought super glue to fix his cut and went straight over to the Grampian bar for a drink , in the Grampian they called him double double, he used to pay his bar tab with a fry of fish.

R.I.P FRANKIE RAEBURN

ROBINA REID
Stanley Robertson used to tell some great stories and was a gentleman and I loved standing next to him at the table and was never bored by him.

RALMOND RICHARDS
You had Freddie Ellis I told him one day that Betty was cutting three fish to your one. And he told me your the gaffer you better tell her lol.

PERCY HUMPHREY
Freddie worked for me, he was only there for the entertainment, the best one was when he cut his nose because he is as blind as a bat.

PATRICK MALONE
You had Billy Stuart he was the white man's Richard Pryor, he was a very funny guy.

STUART CUMMING
The funniest two was big Suds and Brian Strachan down at the market. Billy forsyth was a cracker as well.

MARK MOIR
I used to do a lot of sparky work in George Denny, I recal falling off the top of the kiln which gave all the young lassie's a great laugh.

ROBERT DALGARNO
Good old days long gone ! Remember sending all the trainee salesmen down to Seagear for a long weight

(wait) or for a long stand for a boat ! All the staff at Seagear played along with it. You also had big John Sutherland the antics that him and Brian Strachan got up to on the market floor was unreal, another one was old Abbie Nicol I remember him falling into a huge pile of jumbo skate brie and was covered in it and pretended to swim in it. He would also bid on fish and depending which hand he held up it was either £2.50 or a fiver as he lost half his fingers in a cutting accident years back.

KAZ LONDON
Best job I have ever had was working in the fish... brilliant laughs and no one thought they were better than anyone else.

JAMES EDMOND
For me it was Larry Fettes he was a very funny man and he always looked after me.

LARRY FETTES

One day Denis Barbour took in a new pack of playing cards as they were always playing cards at break times or when waiting for fish. Every one of the cards had pictures of nude women on them and me being the youngest it didn't take much for me to get a red face, so every now and then they would hold up a card and say to me, "What would you do with her?" anyway after a few days the cards went missing and I'm there in this packed bothy, Denis points his finger at me and said, "OK you little perv was it you that stole the cards?" my face went like a beetroot and the sweat started pouring down my face, I must have looked so guilty. Honestly it wasn't me that stole them. Davie leiper our driver started the same day as me and at lunchtime he had to get to the train depot to unload the fish. I asked him if I could go with him during my lunch break, this went on for a few days until Davie asked me why I wanted to spend my lunch break with him unloading fish when I could be relaxing in the bothy. I told him I was so embarrassed after getting the finger pointed at me about the cards.

The train depot was another eye opener for me. The fish lorry's had to be there before 1.30 to unload all there fish into carriages before the train left for Billingsgate fish market in London. Back in the day's that was the only way to get your fish down south. It was a mad rush and if you didn't get there in time you didn't get to unload your fish, even a minute late and you had to wait until the next day which was very costly to the fish merchants as the price of fish might have reduced dramatically the next day.

The guys that worked for the rail wasn't very friendly, you just passed the fish to them and they would pile it up and did not care how they handled your fish, it got that bad that one day Brian Bertram started arguing with one of the rail workers about how he was handling the fish, it got very heated and Brian head butted the guy and ended up in court and was fined £5

Mr Charles Alexander applied for the regrant to himself of existing licences of six operators whose businesses he had acquired. Alternatively he sought one licence to include the nine vehicles belonging to the acquired undertakings. The L.M.S and the L.N.E railway companies objected.

As reflected by the evidence, the case for road transport, from the fish trader's point of view, is as follows ! Fish carried by road is not subjected to so much handling as by rail and door-to-door delivery is provided, it is delivered in better condition. When rail transport is employed there is no guarantee against lass of market, unless the consignment be over 24 hours late, or negligence by the railway company can be proved.

The railway had alleged that Mr Alexander gave false information when he denied carrying fruit from Liverpool to Glasgow. The allegation had been finally withdrawn.

Rail rates were fairly high about 10d per stone gross against 7d by road. The favourable level of road transport rates enables the benefit to be passed on to the consumer. Ice placed on fish carried by rail has to be paid for, whereas haulers provide it free of charge.

Evidence on behalf of Mr Alexander was given by Mr Robert Low a director of Stanley Pibel Ltd a concern of wholesale fish merchants of London and also Mr J Cook manager at Aberdeen Messrs. Mr Cook said that his firm had made many claims against the railway for lost fish. Mr Blumberg director of S. Myrans wholesale fish merchants of Manchester paid high tribute to the efficiency of Mr Alexander's service. He said that the trains from Scotland were sometimes three hours late, but Alexander's vehicles were always punctual, despite the weather.

After dropping off our fish at the train depot sometimes we had to go in past Claben to pick up some half stone boxes of yellow fish and kippers. What a size of place that was. I think half of Aberdeen worked in Claben at some point in their lives.

Claben was owned by Dr Francis Clark and also the Clark family owned "Ben-Line" fleet of trawlers. They were a large fish haulier for their own products and other fish dealers. Their livery was well known around the country whenever the UK fishing fleet was landing fish. They were mostly known for their kippers, they also specialised in smoked cod and haddock. They also supplied wet fresh herring to other merchants, manufacturer's and Canner's, they exported fish to Australia, New Zealand, South Africa, Rhodesia, Kenya. Canada and the United States.

They had their own cold store and quick-freezing plant where temperatures as low as 40 degree could be maintained, also made their own boxes in variety of sizes

Their fleet of transport consisted of 19 vehicles. Ten Mercury H, two Mustangs, and one Mammoth Major, the smaller fleet included four B.M.C, five -tonners, and two seven – ton Thames Traders.

ROBERT SIMPSON

I tipped a lot of herring at Claben as a holiday job on the night shift, then mixed pickle for the start of the day shift. Tough bunch of lassies that worked there, but all with hearts of gold.

Kippering was originally developed as a way to preserve fish in the days before refrigeration, they was prepared by taking fresh herring soaking it in salt water brine and smoking it slowly over a fire composed of oak chips. The big commercial houses have long since abandoned traditional methods so sacrificed the traditional savor, they now add artificial colorings and cut the smoking process from 10-20 hours to only 3 hours now.

1880s shows herring being packed into barrels of salt

In the early 1950s British fishermen were taking more than 100.000 tons of herring a year in the north sea, in 1976 they caught 25.000 tons and at one point the north sea faced possible extinction of herring stock because the Dutch, Danish and British trawlers began using nets with finer mesh, trapping young fish as well as mature ones and the catch plummeted.

After a couple of weeks working at Marine I decided not to go back as I was not learning anything. I didn't tell anyone I wasn't going back. A few weeks of having no job and no money I went to work for two brothers who had a fish-house at the corner of Sinclair road, but that only lasted a few days as one of the brother was very weird and I was told he liked the young boys and to watch myself when I went into the kiln alone with him.

BILLY THOMSON
I worked there and one of them that did the pickling used to spit his false teeth into the dip bucket.

A few days later I was sitting in my bedroom when I heard Jim Wyness shouting up at me, he was up visiting his mum. He asked me why I didn't go back to Marine, I told him the reason, and he said, "Come back on Monday and I will learn you how to fillet". Monday morning off I go again but it was a lot better that time as my two mates Bruce Hawkins and Carl Smith had also started working in the fish, so we all got on the same bus to work. Carl got a job in the arch underneath the bridge peeling prawns, Bruce got a job with Denis and Bosco Adams, the funny stories he used to tell us about the two brothers, Bruce was shit scared of them but he loved working there and they fairly looked after him.

DENNIS ADAMS
I worked for my dad in D&A fish in palmerston place, he was a grumpy fucker lol and my mum also worked there.

Walked back into Marine and what a bad time I got from the workers, calling me a big girl that couldn't handle the fishtrade, but all in good fun. Jim Wyness pulls me aside and told me he had managed to get me a pay rise. When I was a bit older and wiser I realised everything that Jim did for me, but at the time I didn't appreciate what he did for me. I think the reason being...Jim was the gaffer and I always sided with the workers and as always I rebelled against authority. What I did notice when I went back, my pal Davie Leiper wasn't there because they sent him to Peterhead every day to pick up our fish. Our fish from Aberdeen Market was then delivered by father and son Dod and Ronnie Stevens, what a pair they was! Ronnie was the quieter of the two, old Doddie was some guy, most of the time he delivered the fish he was half pissed.

ALAN PIRIE
First time I met Dod was when he reversed into my motor while unloading Billingsgate fish onto Charlie Alexander's motors on the cross market, as he jumped out of his transit to see what he had hit, all the empty cans of Mcewans export started rolling about in the car park, good old days.

STUART CUMMING
Dod and Ronnie were lovely guys, had great banter with them over the years.

Other fish haulers was G&T Frasers, R&J Simpsons, Market transport, and Jim Porters.

G& T FRASERS

R & J SIMPSONS

PORTERS DRIVERS NIGHT OUT

After about a week being back I was then taught how to work the finning machine but I was useless on it. It was a very unsafe and dangerous piece of machinery, many a fish worker lost a finger on that machine.

BILLY SHIRRAN

Myself and my older brother Johnny worked on the finning machines for Ashley Craig, Johnny was seventeen and I was only fourteen at the time. One day my auntie was getting married it was a church wedding then onto the Embassy rooms for the reception party, Ashley said we could have the afternoon off to go but we had to fin off a stock of fish to keep the filleters going. Johnny and myself were going like the clappers and we had about 15 boxes finned, with about fifteen minutes until the filleters got back from their lunch then the inevitable happened, I sliced the corner off my thumb, Ashley drove me up to the hospital in his rolls royce.

I was in there long enough to miss the church service but got home and got washed and dressed for the reception. Not an easy task when your thumb is all wrapped up in thick wad of cotton wool, got to the reception on time for the start of the meal roast beef and all the trimmings and my mother leaning over me to cut up my beaf as I couldn't hold my knife. The fastest boy I seen on a finning machine was Mike Reid when he was at Ashley Craigs. Mike and Jocky Greives used to race each other on that machines.

RALMOND RICHARDS
I have seen lots of good finners in my day but dont know who was the best. It was one of the hardest jobs in the fish industry, it was a eight hour work out if you were picking the boxes up finning them and loading the table as well five days a week every week with no Torry holidays thats a good finner and if you can keep six good filleters going.

COLIN EVANS

I cut the corner of my thumb off on that machine, and they say your not a finner until you do that, still not grown back in yet.

BOB CUSITER

I had a spell with George Denny as a finner unfortunately the filleters mostly woman had other ideas as a young vulnerable boy with little experience in the fish trade. You see finning wasn't my strongest talent as I wanted to keep my fingers intact and didn't really produce the finished product.

After about six months back at Marine I got another pay rise so I must have been doing something right. I also earned a few extra pounds taking the roe out of the fish guts, also when I had nothing to do the filleters would get me to take the cheeks out of the big cod heads as they were worth a few pounds.

COD ROE

I then started to learn how to skin dogfish which wasn't an easy task and was hard graft. You had a long wooden board with a hook attached to it, you would pick up the dogfish which looked like small sharks and hook the mouth of the fish, cut off the fins and then the tails, then cut underneath the belly, cut off the guts, cut the back of the neck then rip the skin off by hand which was like leather. The dogfish was then boxed up and sent straight down to London, the tails were left for days until you filled a three stone box and sent down south, the tails were used for making perfume apparently the stuff off the tails is which made the perfume stick to you, the belly's were skinned and sent to Germany to get smoked and canned up.

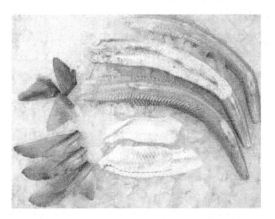

There wasn't a lot of fish merchants who bought dogs at the market for some reason. They were very cheap and sometimes only sold for under £10 a box but was sold down south for a small fortune and Marine made a lot of money just off the dogs.

PERCY HUMPHREY

We used to take the raans out when we were cutting, we would have had about 6-10 stone by the end of the day and got about 10 shillings a stone.

KATE McGREGOR

Working with Jackie Boyd he would boil the raans in the boiler that we got our hot water for our dip, just aswell we had gloves on as our hands would have been stinking.

Couple of years had went by and I still hadn't been taught how to fillet. I wasn't complaining though as I was earning good money. I was fitting in with the staff and giving as good back as I was getting. The fish trade was booming at this time and everybody had plenty of overtime. I loved the overtime because my job was just to tidy up things and go to the chip shop for everyone's supper. The shop I went to was a small chip shop on Walker Place which was owned by the guy that went on to own Mikes fast foods. He made a fortune off the fishtrade lads at night time, I used to go up with my order of maybe 10-20 suppers but would always order one extra for me to eat on the way back to the fish house. Most dinner breaks I would meet up with my mates Carl and Bruce and head off to the Hi Fri cafe at the corner of Palmerston Road. Baker on the way to work, breakfast in the work, cafe at lunch time, and 2 chip shop suppers at teatime, home and have my other supper and i always wondered why I got to the size I am today? Ha ha.

PUBS AND CAFE

During lunch breaks the pubs round about the fish houses were rather busy as many of the fish-workers would nip in for a sneaky pie a pint and a nip. I only did that once myself but many a Friday night after work I would end up in the Rats Cellar or the Grampian bar and still be there at closing time. In those days most workers got their pay weekly, it was all cash in a small brown wage packet and their overtime in another packet. I recall one day I was off sick for a few days and my wife went down to Marine to collect my wages. Stuart Cummings hands her my wage packet and then followed by another packet, she was a bit confused about the other packet until Stuart told her it was my overtime packet. Every week I would go home and hand her my wage packet unopened which she would brag to people about how good I was handing over my whole wages. Little did she know I had my overtime packet hidden in my back pocket. Some Saturday nights I would head down to the Anchorage bar to see Ally Dawson singing upstairs in the lounge, it was very busy in there with mostly people from the fish trade.

Ally was well know for being a bit of a prankster, if a woman went into the toilet Ally would stop singing and without her knowing he would follow her in and put the taps on full and stuck the mike against the running water and then nipped back and started singing, she couldn't understand why everybody was pissing themselves laughing when she came out of the toilet.

ADRIAN NEILLY

I worked in the fish for many years started at D.T Bruce when I was 16, many a tale of going up to the Anchorage or over the bridge to the Grampian and Rats Cellar on a friday dinnertime after wee got our brown envelope with our wages in it, and never went back to work, Ernie Gove would pick me up Saturday morning because he knew I would have still been pissed from the Friday night.

BILLY BRECHIN

I was doing casual work for Larry Fettes in the arches, you started at 6pm and finished at 9pm and got cash in the hand, then everybody went to the Ferryhill Tavern and spent the lot in there, and all got a lift home in the back of the fish lorry.

CAFE

You had the Harbour cafe on Comercial Quay, Rats Cellar cafe, the R.N.M.D.S.F at the corner of Palmerston, Ed and Mary Zanne newsagent and grocer had a cafe in behind the shop, also had the Market kiosk which was run by two lovely ladies before it was took over by Margaret Low the wife of Mike Low of Dunley fish co, they did rolls, pies etc along with lovely hot drinks in a very cold fishmarket. You had Sandy's cafe just at the start of Victoria bridge, Mac's cafe next to the Grampian bar, Commercial cafe bottom of GH Robertsons lane and the Oak tree cafe on Regent road. The most popular one was the Hi Fry cafe as you would get a lovely breakfast. A few fish-houses round that area had no toilets and the workers would nip into the Hi Fry to use their toilets and a cup of tea.

SHARON ANNAND

When I worked in Commercial Quay, we had a man called little Michael who worked with us for over 30 years, he used to go to the Harbour cafe to pick up the milk for our tea and sometimes he would be away for hours, we would always have to send someone to get him and every time he would be sitting yapping to all the fish merchants and getting his breakfast bought for him.

The thing about the fish trade that a lot of people would have not been aware of was the amount of fatalities and casualties was horrendous, many trawler men lost their lives at sea, the casualties was mostly filleters cutting their hands and fingers, also fish bones and fins that would get stuck into your nails which sometimes needed a visit to the Hospital and many a injury regarding the machinery. My first experience with fish poison was when I just started at Marine, they told Davie Leiper to take me to hospital in the fish lorry, he just dumped me there as I would have been there for a few hours, I got my tetanus in the arse and then they let me go, then I realised I had no bus fares and had to walk all the way home with my arse still numb and walking like Norman Wisdom.

LYNETTE ALLAN
Remember when we were cutting cod, well I got fish poison and had to go to hospital and was off work for six weeks.

BUDDY GRAY
I have had bones down my nails hundreds of times my nails are now disfigured and had a lot of poison fingers over the years.

ELIZABETH TAYLOR
I got a fish hook stuck in my little finger, Dod Gray used to hang them up in the changing rooms as he saved them for his fishing. Eric Johnstone took me to hospital and still had my wellie boots on.

After working a few years in the arches for Marine they decided to move into new premises on South Esplanade and turn it into a factory. Some of the staff decided not to go with them and moved to other jobs. The day we moved in, I loved it as it was so modern. They had a couple of offices, proper toilets, changing rooms, canteen, box room, showers etc. The canteen was my favourite of them all as there was no more drinking out of dirty cups and eating off our lap. When we moved in Jim Wynes mother Ina was the tea lady, we used to put our order in on the morning with what we wanted for breakfast and lunch. After a few months, Jim decided to leave and start up his own business and Ina left not much longer after that.

MARINE FISHERIES

Betty Neerie decided to take over her job as the tea lady after working most of her life filleting fish. The people that knew Betty would agree she was one of the nicest people you will ever meet.

BEV, LYNETTE, AND BETTY

After Jim left that's when I started to come out of my shell as Jim was my neighbour and got me the job so I had to be on my best behaviour. Stuart Cummings who was the gaffer at the time got the job as manager and I got the gaffers job, which I think the boss regretted. I was all for the workers and spent most of my time drinking with them every weekend, so it was very hard for me to tell them what to do but I got a lot of respect from them. Some examples was Marine got CCTV installed and the next day I got a ladder and told one of the boys to cover them up with bags. Anytime there was not much doing I would say to them away to the toilets for a cig and read your paper and if they came in with a hangover I would tell them to go have a nap in the box room and I would cover for them. Marine started to expand and get bigger so they started employing more staff and also a couple of new managers which I didn't feel happy about as I had been there for years and in came these new people trying to tell me what to do and starting to show their authority after a couple of days, which didn't go down well with the staff either. As most of you will know that in the fish-trade one day we were very quiet and had nothing to do, the next day you were rushed off your feet and had to get orders out as soon as you could that day or your order was cancelled. That days I would just have to say to the staff... OK folks lets get cracking and get this orders out and every time we did. The times the new managers told them to get the orders out in time they never did. One day we was all in the pub and the new manager asked me why when he told the staff to get the orders out they never managed it, but when I asked them to get the orders out they always did, my reply to him was we are no better than them and if you respect them and look after them they would help you out anytime they could.

Marine started this new guy called Eric Johnstone who was employed to buy, sell and cut skate and was the best in the trade at it, the problem was... Eric was now in charge of me and with me not liking authority I did not get off to a good start with him. I let my chum Val Hutcheon know how I felt about Eric, well Val being Val and says it how it is, me and Val having a cig outside and Eric passes by and Val said to him, "Oh Eric, by the way Mike doesn't like you." After that day me and Eric had a good talk and we got on great after that. I had a lot of respect for Eric and even went drinking out at his place and local a few times. Eric then left Marine to go and start up his very successful business Skateraw.

ERIC JOHNSTONE & MARGARET THATCHER

You had some great bosses and gaffers but also had some horrible ones who treated you like shit.

ELAINE HASTIE
Davie Dalgleish was always good to his staff, used to give you a sub and never took it back off your wages.

LINDA MILNE
Bobby Stalker was one of the best gaffers, he looked after us young ones at magnus grey.

DOD MAIR
Bill Henderson at Sinclair & Robertson, just an absolute toff

SYLVIA BOWDEN
Hendry Keenan fantastic man very caring person and a good laugh.

MOIRA ROBERTSON
There was a few arseholes in the fishtrade, I was fortunate enough to have good bosses.

JAKE FRASER
Harry Foster at Joe Little hard but fair and a true gent.

BOB CRAIG
They all treated you well you wanted for nothing and they always took the time to have a news with you. I first met Herbert Cox when I was sixteen and he always gave us ten bob each for our breakfast, great times great memories and fine folk.

NAMES MENTIONED IN THE GROUP AS GREAT BOSSES AND GAFFERS

Billy Thompson > Jocky Hastie > Graeme Duguid > George Law > Dennis Adams > Tommy Swanson > Freddie Freeland > Gary Wilson > Sandy Norval > TommyWilson > Harry Foster > Davie Christie > Stuart Cummings > Ernie Gove > Bob Morrison > Gordon Greive > Doo Pearson > Eduard Ladwinic > Sonny Pearce

SONNY PEARCE R.I.P

BILLY SHIRRAN

One of the best bosses has to be Roger. Billy Mckintosh, Gordon Fettes and myself were his first employees £17.50 per week 7 till 5, £1 per hour 6 till midnight. Loads of all-nighters at the same rate. Well taken care of by this gentleman, beer provided all the time. Fishhouse was Johansons Greenbank road, fish at that time was provided by J&A Greigs. They also paid my fines or bailed me out during my idiot times. Roger, Billy and Gordon are all sadly gone now but never forgotten.

About a year of moving into the place they started to modernize it. They put in blast freezers which froze your fish in a couple of hours, you would lay your fish on trays and then slide them into a large metal rack then wheel them into the blast freezer, after a couple of hours you would take them out and slam the fish into blue pans and then dip them into a huge tub of water to glaze them and then straight into our coldstore freezer. The reason for the glaze was to stop the fish getting freezer burnt and also it added more weight. Then marine bought the fish house next door which belonged to cox fish as they started to expand even bigger, part of the sale deal was still to let the present occupier still work out of there, there was only two of them and a small table in the corner. They just cut a huge hole in the wall just to get into the place and moved the dog skinning and the skate side of things into there only until they got in a huge tunnel freezer. The tunnel freezer was called the Torry tunnel as it was developed by the Torry research station. We had two girls feeding the tunnel with fresh fish and a guy at the other end filling the pans when they came off frozen and straight into the coldstore.

Then in came the German badder filleting machine which cost them a fortune and was a complete waste of money as it was always breaking down. Marine even sent someone over to Germany to find out all about the machine. Marine bought some crap of machines over the years, they bought a breading machine, we had to get a big plastic drum and pour a few big sacks of flour into it then add water and we used an electric drill with a metal pole attached to it to mix the batter. What a mess we got into as it splattered all over your face and clothes. We poured the batter into the machine followed by a few sacks of breadcrumbs, then feed the fish through the machine. Another trick of the trade was to put them through again just to add more weight. Things started to get more and more complicated as the customers wanted all their frozen fish graded into sizes, we had four girls who had to stand at a small scale all day weighing every fish into separate pans. They then bought a grading machine which again was useless.

LIZ CAMPBELL
I worked in Alex Ross in Tullos and loved it but working on the Torry tunnel was freezing I had chilblains and would stand in a plastic fish box filled with hot water.

DOUGIE McGUIRE
I remember back in the seventies when Mac fish had a badder filleting machine, you had two men at one side taking off the fish heads and another six people trimming the fish, one day we had a bet for £100 who was the fastest to cut ten boxes of cod it was Watty Stevens and myself against the badder machine, we were a £100 richer at the end of the day.

LYN WOOD
Working in Clipper and a cat went through the tunnels and I was crying until the men got it out and heated it up at the electric fire.

JAMES EDMOND
I used to work the band saw for fish steaks and fish fingers in the early seventies at Wm Taylor and son in East Tullos.

CLAIRE SHIRRAN
Myself and Lyn Wood used to work on the tunnels at Marine and Scott prime and sometimes we had to go over to Allen & Dey to use their tunnel, happy days and brilliant memories.

Marine started to concentrate mostly on the frozen fish and stopped the dog fish and skate, very rarely did they put out any fresh fish. It was all food safety and hygiene after that and beginning to take the fun side out of the job. No more having a cig when you wanted also stupid hair nets etc. We started to get a smoke break every hour and we had to go outside to have it. One day I was outside having a cig when I noticed Aberdeen's Willie Miller driving slowly past me with his window open, me for a laugh shouted, "Hey Willie, do you want a fry o fish?" well, the brakes went on and he said, "Yes, I wouldn't mind" I nipped in and got him about half o stone of haddocks. Another well known name that came in for a fry was Bobby George the darts player, he was playing a darts exhibition that was on at the White Cocade that night. Speaking of visitors, most fish houses had them on a daily basis, you could have bought anything from shoes to mattresses, loads of dodgy sellers back in them days.

PERCY HUMPHREY
The Polish watches was the best, you bought them and then went straight up to Market street to pawn them, paid ten shillings for them and pawned them for a pound.

AUDREY McGREGOR
I remember when the Polish trawlermen came round selling shirts and lighters.

We started to get really busy and there was plenty of overtime going, some days I was working from 6am till 8pm, also most weekends. Sometimes we would do all nighters until they started a permanent night shift.

Marine was placed in the middle of Cables and Murrays lane, next door was Bobby Geddes and across from us was Harry Leith.

SUSAN BUCHAN
I worked with Bobby Geddes with Danny Main, Podger, Jim, Bob and Gary Knowles, Davy and Watty Stevens, Liz Taylor and little Frankie who has been my partner for 37 years, Sonny Fettes place was next to ours.

GRAEME COOPER
Ashley Craig, Jocky Grieve, then Patchy Leiper and at the top was Duguids and at the bottom was Cod supply, JimWhite Alba fish, Gary Wilsons Grampian,and Brian Sunley

NORMAN SINCLAIR
I worked for a time with Jonny Thomson in Cables lane inside Leipers fishhouse, the people there were the nicest and kindest people I have ever came across.

STEPHEN ANDERSON
My father Ivan Anderson worked in Mowatts in Cables lane all his days, he was the smoker, I also worked in the summer holidays for Theron.

After working for Marine for 14 years I decided to call it a day. I started to get out of hand drinking at weekends, getting myself into trouble and sometimes getting locked up until Monday. I didn't think I was being fare, as Stuart never gave me any warnings about having the 'Torry holiday' off every other week and I felt as I was starting to take the piss. Stuart Cummings was such a great friend and a great gaffer except for one day he tried to pull a fast one on me and Davie Leiper. Davie and myself followed Aberdeen every week and when they reached the quarter-final of the European cup winners cup against Bayern Munich we were all set to book our tickets, Stuart turns round and said to me "Mike we both can't take time of to go to Germany as one of us has to stay and look after the fish-house" I wasn't happy he then said, " look I will go to Germany and if we reach the final you and Davie can go to it" I know he was thinking that Aberdeen would have never got to the final! They did and off we went to Gothenburg and Stuart was as sick as a parrot lol.

STUART CUMMING

MARINE STAFF

THE FISH

In the 1790s it was recorded that there were 36 men from Torry engaged in fishing in 6 boats. By the mid 19th century this had fallen to 3 boats with 6 men in each of them. Despite the temporary fall in numbers the fish caught were the same : haddock was fished in January and May; cod, ling and turbot were caught at a distance of ' several league's from the land and herring was fished from the middle of July. Steam powered trawlers transformed the fishing industry from the 1880s and had a significant impact on Torry. Herring is served in numerous ways, raw, fermented, pickled, cured or smoked as kippers. The herring from the boat to the shores were known as "quarter crans" and carried the official brand of certification, each barrel of gutted and salted herring would contain between 1000 to 1200 herring depending on the grade of the herring. The barrels for white herring were made of Norwegian birch and ash, while the barrels for the red or smoked herring were made of fir.

A BUSY DAY AT POINT LAW, ABERDEEN.

During the medieval period Aberdeen was famous for it's sweet red salmon. Today many firms carry on this ancient and honourable trade. The firm of John Ross jr started as a salmon-smoking business in 1857, it exported it's salmon to 38 countries. Most of it's fish is smoked in the traditional way in the old brick kilns, and much of the preparation work, including filleting and salting is still done in the time-honoured fashion by hand. The firms brick kilns have been used for over 150 years. In February 2008 Historic Scotland designated two of their ovens as category b listed buildings. John Ross is one of the last remaining smokehouses to create smoked salmon the way that it used to taste.

In my days in the fish-trade the most common fish you would have seen in the fish-houses were haddock, cod and whiting. Cod remains an important fish for Scottish fishermen. In the 1970s and 1980s some very large landings were made. Today cod is no more than a small but valuable catch to the Scottish demersal fleet.

Cod accounts for only 2.7% of the tonnage of all fish and shellfish landed into scotland by uk vessels. Two main stocks of cod (the north sea and west of scotland) contributed to scottish landings in 2008 of 7,645 tonnes worth just over 16 million. Small catches are also made at Rockall. A variety of types of trawl nets are used to catch cod mainly in offshore areas at present. In the past inshore fisheries and local 'set net' fishing have been important today, however they are no longer pursued. Whole cod range from 500g to over 6kg with the smaller fish 500g and under are sometimes known as codling.

Haddock is the most important demersal fish species to Scottish fishermen. There are three stocks of haddock, north sea, west coast and rockall which contribute to Scottish landings. In 2008 approximately 29,500 tones of haddock were landed into Scotland, worth 32.7 million. Haddock accounts for around 35% of all demersal whitefish landings into Scotland. The north sea fishery is by far the most significant; around 90% of haddock is landed into the north sea ports. Haddock is part of the cod family, but doesn't grow as large, and is not usually available beyond 3.5 kg, the flesh is not as white as cod and is not as flaky, but has a slightly sweeter taste, which is why haddock is the best whitefish for smoking. Finnan haddock is cold smoked haddock representative of a regional method of smoking with green wood and peat in north east scotland. The origin is the subject of a debate, as some sources attribute the origin to the hamlet of Findon, Aberdeenshire.

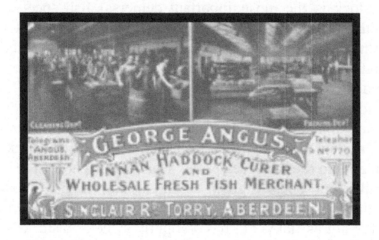

Whiting is a smaller fish from the cod family, with a silvery-grey body and rounded belly, and rarely found over 2kg. This is often an overlooked fish but like Coley. Whiting fillets are mostly a block fillet rather than a single fillet and very nice when fresh but can easily be overcooked.

Very few fish houses catered for flatfish such as place,

witches,dabs, skate, and also the two most expensive
fish in the market, lemon sole and halibut only because
they were so scarce, a box of lemon sole would sometimes
treble the amount of any other box of fish. If a halibut
came into the fish market it would sell for crazy money.

ROBERT DALGARNO

*I used to love selling halibut caught by the long liners,
biggest I ever sold was 20st plus, a guesstimate was 25st,
the market scales only weighed up to 20st. The liners used
to catch well over a hundred of them.*

PATRICK McGUIRE

*Caught plenty of halibut when I was on the Fairtry 2, at
fishing grounds known as the Gully's south end of the
Newfoundland banks in the Atlantic, if we caught a ton of
halibut we got paid for two, at that time we got
approximately 12 shillings the ton, it was always a double
bonus.*

JACQUELINE HUNTER

*When I started in the fishtrade in the sixties I saw a
halibut nearly the size of a small fish house when I
worked in Danny Buchan, probably a rare occurrence to
see a large halibut now because of the overfishing etc.*

GEORGE LEIPER

*Joined the Caledonia in Vestmannayer in 1968, and did a
33 day trip to get home to Aberdeen, sometimes it took
three of us with big gaffs to get the halibut on deck.*

Sometimes on rare occasions when tipping a box of haddock or cod into the filleters table at the bottom would be a flat fish in amongst them. Well... as quick as lightning, hands would come across from the filleters trying to grab it first. I have witnessed many of argument between filleters over this. It was a case of, I seen it first or you got the last time.

Lemon Sole is a right-eyed flatfish with a small head and mouth and smooth slimy skin, the upper surface is reddish brown in colour, mottled with pink and orange with flecks of yellow and green, and a prominent orange patch is typically found behind the pectoral fin, the underside is white, and can reach lengths of up to 65 centimetres.

HALIBUT

When I left Marine I went to casual for Kenny Allen and Dick Gribble who had hired a table in Doo Pearsons place in Cables lane. This was a very common thing back then. You would hire a table in a fish merchants building for around a £100 a week and fill your table with casual filleters (people that was claiming social security) and working for extra cash filleting. The person that hired the table would approach fish merchants and ask them if they had too much fish, if so they would cut them for a stoneage fee, I think the going rate for medium size fish was about £1.20 per stone, and then they would pay their casual workers about 90p per stone, on top of that they would make a lot of money from their fish manure.

When I first started in the fish they would fill round metal barrels with fish bones and guts and when they were filled you had to roll them outside and leave them there until the manure lorry would come around once or twice a day and empty your barrels.

A few years later UFP fishmeal changed their way of collecting your fish manure, they would dump large yellow plastic tubs outside the fish-house. The filleters had to throw their bones into plastic bins and as soon as they were filled the labourer would come along with his hook and pull them outside and empty them into the yellow tubs. UFP would then arrive once a day and load them onto their truck with a forklift.

The good thing for me working for Kenny and Dick was that most of their fish they cut was for Marine, Stuart Cummings told them that they had to pay me the full amount of stonage or they would not be getting anymore fish from Marine, which they both agreed on. Most of the fish we cut was small haddocks and small codling, and our table was nearly all single fillet cutters. Doo Pearsons staff who mostly all was block filleters. Derek (doo) Pearson who was a Northfield lad started his own business at an early age with Jim (kyzer) Mckay but after a while they went their separate ways and Doo moved into premises in Cables lane. I remember working away at our table and after the fish market was over Doo would appear have a look around, go upstairs to get changed and down grafting away for the rest of the day sometimes working until 8pm. For being a small guy he used to unload boxes upon boxes of fish off of the trucks and I'm not surprised he went onto being a very successful fish merchant and also the owner of a few great horses. His success was partly down to his foreman Gordon Tait R.I.P who worked for Doo for 28 years.

BOB CRAIG
Gordon was a toff of a guy I delivered fish into doo's often Gordon was a tall guy and he could unload your motor in minutes.

ROY MALCOLM
A nicer man than Gordon you will never meet.

ANDREW MORTIMER
I remember moving a massive table from Dalglishes to Doo's place in Cables lane and was wearing my good dress jacket, never wore that jacket again. The gold cup where Doo won it with the horse Regal Parade my whole family had it on at 66/1 as we knew it was a good one. Doo used to stand outside the bookies at 12 years old asking people to put his bets on.

Doo has had about 70 winners in dab hand racing and also two million in prize money with his horses. A few of us fish-workers made a few pounds backing his horses. One was called the Tatling, a horse that had it's knees held together by pins and bolts and used to run like a crab but earned him and his partner Alan Pirie lots of prize money.

DEREK (doo) PEARSON

It had the bookies in the Granite city ducking for cover when bionic sprinter the Tatling landed the group 2 King's stand stakes at Royal Ascot. They bought the seven year old gelding with the wonky legs from a Catterick claimer for 15,000, but the Tatling blossomed under the tender care of trainer Milton Bradley who has enhanced his reputation for improving horses.

His fish business is still going strong and has still got some of his staff that was with him when he started up all those years ago.

After working with Kenny and Dick for a few months I decided to go on my own, and that's when the fun started. I rented a small table in Sheila Thompsons place over in the arches, I think there was only three of us Alan Riddell, Terry and myself. We was getting a small amount of fish from Marine just to keep us ticking over, I was signing on at that time, and was just making some extra cash for my beer money. Couple of weeks later Kenny and Dick had called it a day and now Marine was looking at me to take on all their work. Within a week I managed to fill an eight man table and everyone of them was on the social, and signing on like myself. One of my filleters was a guy called Dod Herd and what a man he was. Dod was like myself, well overweight we used to give each other abusive compliments all day but all in good fun. In them days you only had to shout one word ! (SOCIAL) and you have never seen so much Usan Bolts take to their heels. One day me and Alan was arriving back from the fish-market and just as we pulled into the car-park outside our place we couldn't believe our eyes, the social had raided our place. All the guys came running out of the fish-house still with their boots and aprons on and started running up the steep hill next to the fish house followed by the social, next minute the social stopped in their tracks and were hysterically laughing watching Dod Herd trying to run up this hill and they ended up jumping in their car and called it a day.

WILLIAM SMITH
I went to sign on one day and the woman said to me " what a smell of fish, have you been working" I said " no I have just passed about ten fish houses looking for a job.

AUDREY McGREGOR
I was working away one day on the skinning machine, turned round to pick up a tray of fish and was talking to myself because everyone was hiding as we just got raided by the social. A certain fish merchant would call the social to grass off a few fish houses who was hiring guys who was on the social, but it backfired on him as the social said to him, " we might aswell check your place since we are here" they came across one of his workers had been signing on for six years while working for him.

DOUGIE McGUIRE
I was working in the arches on a ten man table, social turned up and only two people was left cutting, as the rest took to their heels.

COLLEEN McGUIRE
You hired a table in our place in Michingle road, social came in and I have never seen anyone run so fast, one of your filleters even hide in the chill.

You always knew when one of the filleters had to sign on, as they would have came to work with a change of clothes and a tin of deodorant or a bottle of perfume.

Even though it was hard graft working in the fish, it was a

laugh a minute. Every time you went to the pubs around the fish area, there was a new and funny story to be told about things that some of the workers got up to that day.

DOUGIE McGUIRE

One day I was sitting in the Ferryhill pub, and in walks Freddie Ellis with his front door, I said to him "Hi freddie why have you got a front door with you" Freddie said " the wife threw me out and she said if you can find anything with your name on it, you can have it, so I took the door as it had my name on it.

PERCY HUMPHREY

My manager Charlie Scott at John Bruce in 1965 said to me " Percy go down to Charlie Taylors and ask for a long stand and don't come back until you get it" so I went into the bar and had a long stand and went back two hours later and said to Charlie " sorry he has run out of it, but said come back tomorrow.

ARLEEN McDONALD

Someone put my daughter Hayley to the end of the factory in Alec Ross for a long stand and left her standing for 20 minutes, and they all ripped into her after that.

ELAINE HASTIE

I remember when I fell down the drain and was up to my head in pickle as jimmer took the cover off the draine for a laugh.

COLLEEN McGUIRE

When we worked for Freddie Fraser and Alex Stopper was the gaffer, Bobby Flood's son worked there, they were both very big drinkers and would drink cans of beer whenever nobody was looking, but there were never any empty tins to be seen. Our bothy was getting a makeover because their was something wrong with the walls and floor, a hole was made in the wall which was directly above the chill, when they got on top of the chill to fix the hole all they could see was hundreds of empty tins of beer.

John Law who I worked with, used to nip up to Burtons cloths shop every friday for a new rig out because he wanted to go out drinking after work with us, and he knew if he went home to get changed first his wife would not have let him out. A few of the workers had booked a couple of days off to go down to Blackpool, but Johns wife said he couldn't go, that night he got so drunk he jumped on a train to Blackpool, once he sobered up and realised where he was he jumped into a taxi to get him home at the cost of £200.

It was my 40th birthday party at the Metro and my sisters son who was only 13 couldn't go because it was over 18s only. His father Chris Jones who was Freddie Frasers gaffer at the time, had to baby sit him, well he had other ideas, he painted a moustache on him and some eyeliner to make him look older and then took him up to the Metro for my party, and both got in no bother as he was very tall for his age.

PATRICK MALONE

I remember working for Mike and one day we were very busy and two filleters went away for their lunch break, but forgot to come back, and only to be found sitting by the Banks of the Dee pissed, when they decided to come back that day they went up the stairs to get changed, only for them both to get a smack on the face and given £20 each and told to come back early the next day.

PERCY HUMPHREY   COLLEEN McGUIRE

PATRICK MALONE   DOUGIE McGUIRE

After the raid by the social we had to look for another new fish merchant to rent a table from. Our next move was over to Midshingle road where we rented a table from Kyzer. We was starting to get very busy then and I had to get more filleters in which was so easy to do as a good bulk of the fish workers were on the social. The place started to get a bit crowded, and there wasn't enough room to swing a cat but we was so grateful just to have a place. Then one day again, we got raided. The reason they kept finding us was because at that time, it was a cut throat business and if you stepped on someone's toes all they had to do was pick up the phone and report us to the social. What I found was the people that reported us were doing the same thing as us and didn't like the fact we were either stealing their workers or getting fish from their suppliers. That was us on the move again, with more workers and a few more pounds in my pocket I was able to get a bigger place of our own. We moved into Doo Pearsons old place in Cables lane and doubled the amount of filleters, as we were getting fish from everywhere but Marine was still our priority, our next big supplier was Polarfish also Jocky Grieve and a few others. I never liked cutting fish for Polarfish, the reason being... I was always out of pocket because we cut his fish in the afternoons and they didn't collect them until the next day, so when the filleters weighed their fish I paid them for that weight as they worked on a stonage rate and because the fish had been lying out all night the water would drain out of them. When the fish got back to Polarfish they weighed every pan which was lighter than the day before, they knocked money off my bill. Another trick of the trade by the stonage filleters was to add water to their pans of fish to get more weight.

We started to get a name for ourselves as we had over twenty filleters and some of the fastest filleters in the trade. Everyone of them on the social, it was only a matter of time before we got another visit from them. I started to worry about getting caught so I got myself a guy to do my accounts and he advised me to start going legit. I had a meeting with all the workers about it and told them I would have to start putting them all through the books, but everyone of them said no chance as they would all leave. People reading this might think what a cheek, signing on and making extra cash, but to be fair in this game you were never guaranteed work, it was always a feast or famine. It was different if you were a fish merchant as you had your daily customers orders and could afford to put their staff through the books, but with what we did, we only cut fish for people if there was an overflow of fish in the markets, sometimes we could have went weeks without any work.

Over the years you had some great and fast filleters, the fast ones were mostly on stonage and also you had good filleters who could get all the flesh off of the bone which was important for the merchants that dealt with the larger fish.

BOB CRAIG

Davie Wood that worked for Donald Leiper in Midchingle road was one of the best single filleters in the town, he was put forward for a best filleter in uk award which was held in Scarborough up against filleters from Grimsby, Hull and Feetwood.

ELIZABETH GRAY

I can't say for sure who was the best sole filleter, but my sister in law Lottie Leonard r.i.p was brilliant absolutely clean bone well scraped and fast with it.

STUART CUMMING

Jim Wyness best cod cutter every fillet a beauty and he was fast. You had Alex (plum) smith, young John Bruce all beautiful and fast. Pearl Chalmers was a fantastic plaice cutter.

Like father like son, Mark Smith who works for Colin Fraser and who now is classed as one of the top filleters in Aberdeen, just like his father Plum Smith r.i.p. I worked with Plum for many a years and what a toff of a guy he was, he was taken from us at such an early age.

GORDON GRIEVE

Andy Garden, Fred Greig best sole filleters, Nanny Turner at block filleting or Raymond Charles, Billy Sinclair best cod filleters, Becky Pearce was a lovely block filleter no bones every fillet was a topper for presentation.

EDWARD FLETCHER

My mother Gina Fletcher was a yield cutter and quality looking fillets ! She had the reputation that she could get weight out of a box of matches. I'm not a speed sole filleter but i'm a quality filleter that prides myself on getting max yield and trained by the best my mother.

BILLY SHIRRAN

My youngest brother Sandy can't be very far off the fastest and cleanest single filleters that I can remember watching I believe that Percy Humphrey's gave him the nickname (Flashing Blade). I was brought up working in the fish trade from a very young age, I was fortunate to have cut soles alongside Andy Ewen, Sonny Pearce, and Andy Garden to name a few. Singles with Gordon Fettes, Dod Mackintosh and Frankie Raeburn. Blocks I can do but was not my forte.

SANDY SHIRRAN

ALEXANDER LESLIE

I think my dad was one of the best dog skinner in Aberdeen, he was the one that showed how to skin dogs on a board, as he was showed how by a Danish fisherman in Aberdeen harbour, everyone was still doing it the old way.

As far as I'm lead to believe, stonage filleting for cash in hand started back in the sixties at Rutherfords also Starwood, Larry Little, Ashley Craig and Alex Gove. There was even a filleting school back then, it ran three month courses in all aspects of fish processing. Some other top filleters were Billy Stewart / Raymond Steel / Charlie Simpson / Eileen Gill / Big Dykes Wood / Raymond Walker / Irene Fettes / Christine Robertson / Arthur Esson / Mary Duff / Sylvia Cox / Fred Greig / Danny Main / Duncan Rose / Brian Sunley / Percy Humphrey / Graeme Cooper. The name that kept coming up as the best block filleter was Buddy Gray.

BUDDY GRAY

We had some laughs in the fish, I worked for over 40 years and loved it so much we had laughs and fights too but some lovely people to work with. I miss getting my fry of fish every week . I started of as a packer then a skinner then filleter, I worked for Joe Little, Ashley Craig, Alex Gove, Jockey Grieve, and loads more and ended in H and H fish for 12 years and made the most money at John Laws. Some great times I remember the time when I went to the toilet, the door had a big hole in it and someone threw a pigeon in while I was having a pee I near fainted and had a good laugh about it. Another time I had to go home from work as I was ill, when I walked out of the fish house the burger van was there and decided to have pie and chips, started walking along the road eating my chips and got to the bottom of Market Street and just about to eat my pie and all of a sudden a bird shit on my pie, I started crying walking up market street with people looking at me and wandering what I was crying for. When some of my old workmates meet up we still have a laugh about that day.

During our time working in Doo Pearsons old place it was great in the summer time, we was getting plenty of fish and having such a laugh as we was all making good money, we even had a bed and a fruit machine in there. The bed was for anyone that got thrown out by their wife lol I got thrown out plenty of times but wouldn't sleep there as I was terrified of mice. The money I made off the fruit machine paid for the rent of the premises, come pay day on a Friday they would all get cash in hand and I made sure I gave them some coins in their wage packet as I knew they would spend it all on the fruit machine. One week Gavin D spent all his wages on the machine but I opened up the machine and gave him all his money back. We even had a tea lady which was Ronnie smiths grandmother and such a lovely woman.

The biggest problem we had at that time was getting the workers into work early and also when we had cut all the fish, we sometimes had to wait hours for the fish to be picked up. The way I solved that problem was, I used to be the manager of a Sunday league football club and had the same problem getting the players to the game on time. My mind started working overtime and thought of an idea to kill two birds with one stone. I said to my players, "What about we buy a second hand mini bus out of our funds?". The first week we had our bus and before the football team had been in it I was taking all the fish workers in it every day, to make it even worse rather than wait for our fish to be picked up we would deliver it in the bus. Come Sunday morning picking up the players the bus was stinking of fish and they wasn't very happy with me, Even up until this day they still bring it up about the stinking mini bus. Come the winter months it was getting very gloom as we was hardly getting any fish but bills had to be paid like renting gas heaters, electric, rent etc, also the workers started to leave as there was nothing doing. Alan Riddel and myself was down at the fish market at six every morning asking merchants if they wanted any fish cut but nothing doing. After a few months I decided to call it a day and sold all my tables and everything in the fish house.

After years of working in the fish this was my first experience of life down at the fish market, and it was an eye opener for me to see how much hard work goes into things down there before the fish reaches our fish houses and it just fascinated me.

The Association was established in may 1888, as Aberdeen fish trade association, and was incorporated with its present title in 1944. It began in response to the introduction of sales by auction in the late nineteenth century, its first achievement being an agreement amongst fish sellers to provide discounts for cash sales to accredited buyers. The purpose of this agreement was to put the fish trade of Aberdeen on a more firm and substantial footing with regard to the paying of fish bought on the pier' and in particular to exclude the large number of bogus buyers who had not the means to pay for what they were bidding for, harassing the legitimate buyers and putting the trade in a very bad condition. Prior to Aberdeen establishing itself as the oil and gas capital of Europe, the fishing industry was the predominant sector in the city. Aberdeen flourished as a major fishing port throughout the 19th and 20th centuries with the construction of the old fish market along Commercial Quay in 1889.

The port established itself as Scotland's leading whitefish port due to its large trawling fleet and equally large processing sector. August 1969 striking trawler-men were held behind a barricade at the fish-market during a ten-week strike over wages. Palmerston quay was remodelled in the 70s which seen a new fish market and opened by the Queen. Thousands of tons of gravel reclaimed a corner of Albert Basin from the sea, steel pilling outlined the shape of the new quay which was scheduled for completion in 1976.

Sales were stopped for a special auction at the market in July 1979. Merchants and skippers forgot about the business on the market floor as the bidding started for a football with the autograph of one of the best-known names in football – Jock Stein, Scotland's manager. Aberdeen fish merchant Gordon Cowie took the ball with a bid of £130.

Adverts and information adorned the outer wall of the market to inform the public of the fish species landed. The Quay deck surface was scored for ease of drainage and improving foothold. Undersize fish landed would be condemned for fishmeal use, only to discourage future catches of small fish and preserve the rising fishery stocks from further plunder. During the heyday of the market, it wasn't unusaul for the floor area to fill up with boxes 3 times, the trawlers were lined up 2 and 3 deep ready to have their haul unloaded. Experienced lumpers would be down in the hold filling baskets which were attached to a crane pulley system, and hauled up to the quay floor. The men on the quayside would pack the fish into the 1cwt boxes ready for the business that day. Everyday there was an inspection by the Government Department of fish and Agriculture also the staff from the research laboratory and would appear in their shiny white boots and sparkling white coats, they would measure, weigh and take a small sample back to their lab for testing. The lumpers would tease them about getting their hands dirty, and tell them to get a real job, but they did a necessary service to the industry and no-one resented them.

MARINE LAB TORRY

Also other men that wore the white coats was the Auctioneers, usually each buyer had a regular order for what fish to buy. The auctioneers knew who wanted haddock, cod, mackeral, etc and could anticipate the raising of the eyebrow or the slight movement of a shoulder or hand which indicated a bid. The buyers would stand around the catch which was on offer staring at the boxes shuffling their feet,waiting for the salesman to call Sold. Then the buyer would slap their identity tickets on the boxes and then move on to the next lot.

The tickets were there for the drivers to know which boxes to hook out and load onto their lorry and taken back to their fish houses.

They also had a kiosk in the market and was used to receive phone calls from different fish businesses to let their buyers know to contact their office, they would announce it over their tannoy system, most of the time it was to let the buyers know that they had just received more orders from their suppliers. Previously it would have been the job of a young boy to get on his bike, pedal like mad to the market and try to find his contact to pass on the message, which was a hit or miss way of conducting business. When the buyer heard his name on the tannoy he made a dive for the nearest telephone box which many were sited the length of the market, to get his new instructions.

ROBERT DALGARNO

I was an auctioneer that started with Alan in Don fishing co, then B.U.T/ Caley fisheries, David Whyte then P&J Johnstone. Great days dealing with so many characters, some good and some bad. My dad Bill Dalgarno was a well know face in the market back in the late 40s until the 70s. He was a boxman and worked for Mannofield fishing company and John Wood & Son. His job was to get the trawlers ready for the porters to land their catch, he also had to make sure the boat was ready in time for the next trip. My granda Sandy also worked in the market looking after the long liners for Malcolm Smith. There was a guy there called big Suds what a comedian and such a nice guy, he used to catch the newbies out with the old perfume trick of getting them to smell his jacket where a lady had supposedly splashed perfume all over it, then gave them a kiss when the leant towards him, he also used to pretend to be gay in front of tourists by walking and skipping through the market, holding hands with Brian Strachan. There were two lovely ladies that worked in the market kiosk, one did the announcements over the tannoy and served hot drinks, the other lady acted as a tourist guide.

GRAHAM HEPBURN

I was so nervous on my first day at the market but Suds made it a lot better by flashing a scribble on his note book that said " I love you" when no one else was looking.

MIKE POCOCK

Great banter in those days, big Johns daughter and her

CLABEN STAFF NIGHT OUT

LIZ MACRAE

I remember having to pick up a basket of kippers every Thursday night when I lived in the childrens home saint Martha's on the spital, round about 1964-67. the workers used to give me a penny to get sweets, what a lovely bunch.

CHARLIE GORDON GAFFER AT CLABEN

piano lessons, was another wind up from him.

GORDON FALCONER

Remember buying 500 boxes of cod in one shot, was working for Bobby Geddes at the time.

COLIN EVANS

I was a tally boy for years on the market, loved having my breakfast in the harbour cafe. Ian Wood now Sir Ian Wood was running down the market and slipped and fell right on his arse, it was the biggest cheer I have heard in the market. Also the time when the BBC and ITV were there for the opening of the Tilt bridge, Jim Porters lorry's got there early and all lined up to make sure George T Frasers lorry's couldn't get in any of the camera shots and pictures.

PERCY HUMPHREY

I would go with my dad 3 or 4 in the morning at the age of nine to give him a hand cutting the dogfish.

JOHN HORNE

I remember one xmas when we were still above the bookies next to the Anchorage pub, the Market Police used to come into our office for a drink, that day we had run out of drink so one of the policemen put on one of our white coats then went down to the pub to buy a carry out, and came back up the stairs to our office to have a drink with us.

PAULINE HOWIE

My dad, my granda and great granda were all fish market

porters, also my uncle and great uncle and cousins were all fish market porters. My dad and granda would always say to me that when I reach 21 I would be the first female fish porter. I used to love getting up early during the school holidays, when my dad was off too, he would take me down to the market to see all the fish in the boxes from one end to another. I also got to see a giant squid just casually lying in ice at the side. The fish market children's Christmas parties and disco were brilliant, I was known as the lemon sole kid lol.

ROBERT DALGARNO   COLIN EVANS

PAULINE HOWIE   MIKE POCOCK

Harbour police man Terry Brown and police cadet Marie Rennie share a joke with Peter Ross, a buyer for James Wood

Manager of Trawl-Pac Davie Burns

After a few months away from the fish-trade and still with no job and no money I had no option but to go and find myself a job back in the fish-trade. I got myself a job with Frankie Hildreth cutting small fish on stonage. A few of the guys that worked for me was working there now. Frankie was some guy and didn't take shit from no one and a lot of guys were scared of Fankie because he would go off on one every now and then but when you got to know him Frankie was a good guy. I got on great with Frankie, he used to pick me up from my house in the mornings and would talk to you as a friend rather than a boss on the way to work. One day a certain filleter never turned up for work so Frankie drove up to his house walked right in went up the stairs and dragged the person clean out of his bed. Filleters never stayed long at Frankie's because the fish he would get in was so small and sometimes took you all morning to cut just four stone of fish. Sadly one morning I was working away and we was told that Frankie had passed away the night before.

I then decided to start up on my own again, so off I went again trying to rent a small fish house, I managed to get one in Cable's lane and what a dump of a place, but better than nothing. Went to see Stuart at Marine to see if I could start cutting fish for them again, he started us off with a few boxes a day just to keep us going. After a few months the fish was very cheap to buy from the market and most merchants couldn't buy them as they did not have enough filleters, so every morning I had merchants coming up to me asking if I could cut their fish, but I would only cut fish for them if Marine didn't have a days work for us.

One day in the market we got the shock of our lives when Junior Bellamy who had a huge factory up in Mintlaw approached me and asked if I could handle a large amount of fish for him on a daily basis. It was too big of an opportunity to turn him down, even when I knew marine would not be happy about it, but like the saying 'never put all your eggs in the same basket'. Next morning he gave us seventy boxes, also fifty boxes from marine and a few boxes from other merchants. I had enough table space for twenty one filleters and filled the spaces in no time. More filleters were coming in asking for a job and getting more fish than I could handle, so decided to start a night shift and filled the twenty one spaces at night. Then I started to panic again as I had forty two people working for me and every one of them was casual and cash in hand. Thinking if I get caught I could end up in jail this time but I was in too deep and I think the greed got the better of me. I was making a lot of money from the fish manure alone let alone the thirty pence a stone off every filleter. With the high volume of fish I was cutting the fish manure was also very high volume and decided to sell my manure to Noble's of Fraserburgh because they paid more than anyone else and also he paid you monthly, the only snag was we had to go up to Fraserburgh and get the cheque from him so we could cash it at his bank. Every Friday we also had to go to Bellamys in Mintlaw to get a cheque from him to cash it at his bank on that day. We would drive up with a car load of us on Friday morning cash the cheque then in the pub for our breakfast while the workers were in the fish-house waiting for us to come back with their wages.

On a Friday the workers wasn't to keen to do any work as

they had put in so many hours all week so I tried to avoid taking in any fish on a Friday. Some Fridays when we didn't have to go to Mintlaw, a few off us would sneak up early mornings to Balnagask for a game of golf, knowing fine a few smaller merchants would hit us with a small amount of fish, and we couldn't be bothered getting changed for a few hours work, and knew the workers that was in waiting for their wages would have to get changed and cut the fish, as they thought we were up in Mintlaw.

One day I will never forget, it was a Friday morning Alan Riddell and myself headed down to the fish market and could not believe the amount of fish that was landed that day, at least a thousand boxes of medium haddocks, right away Junior Bellamy approached us and asked us how much we could handle, we said a few hundred...two minutes after that Stuart Cummings came running up to us and asked us the same question, we didn't like to tell him Junior had approached us first, so we said we will manage a few hundred. We knew because it was a Friday and there was so many fish which had to be filleted over the weekend and not many fish merchants would buy that amount of fish on a Friday, we knew the fish was going to be very cheap to buy that day. Alan and myself went away for our breakfast only to be told when we got back to the market that Junior had bought 400 boxes for us and Marine had got us 200 boxes. I started to panic as we had no where to store that amount of fish. Simpsons transport loaded up Bellamys fish and said they would leave their truck parked outside our place over the weekend to help us out. The busiest day of my life, I said to Alan I had to nip home for something and would be right back. That week I had just bought myself a new car and nipped home and told the wife to start packing as we are off to Blackpool. We went to the school and made an excuse about how I had to take the kids home, then an hour later we was on our way to Blackpool, went in to the service cafe at Preston and decided to give Alan a phone, when he picked up the phone he said " where to fuck are you as you said you would be back in an hour" when I said Preston and on my way to Blackpool for the weekend he was not a very happy man lol. Came back on Monday and all 600 boxes had been filleted.

THE FISH MERCHANTS

My years in the fish trade what I did notice was that every other week you would hear of someone starting up their own business, some would go on to be very successful and still going strong today but a large percent of the people that did start up on their own did not last very long, I never knew the reason for it, was it because they had some good financial people behind them to see them through the hard times? Was it because of the contacts they had or was it just plain hard graft and had a good business head on them? Which, in my opinion was the latter of the three. Some of the fish companies in Aberdeen have been established for over one hundred years now. Also back in my days every now and then you would hear of a fish-house that went on fire during the night, the rumours were that some of them was an insurance job but never proven so maybe just speculation.

You have Allen & Dey which was established in 1890 and has been a major influence in the development of fish processing and trading in Scotland, they have continued to respond to the ever changing demands of a constantly changing seafood industry, in its ability to adopt both to availability of species and customer trends. While trading in fresh,frozen,smoked and shellfish products, they dominated in a range of Scottish salmon products. This was a logical development from many years as a player in the growth of the Scottish farmed salmon industry.

IRENE ROBERTSON
My best years was working in allen & dey for twenty years, loved every minute of it, what I liked was if you had kids they let you off for the school holidays without paying you off, like some firms would.

ROBERT DALGARNO
I think they bought J.C Spence out of the premises he had.

JAMES EDMOND

I supplied a lot of fillets to Allen & Dey in the 70s and 80s a great old established company, and many merchants like myself were glad to trade with them.

DENISE DOWNIE

My dad went up to Kinlochbervie a lot to collect salmon for Allen & Dey, I used to go with him sometimes, he also went to Helmsdale in his fish lorry.

EXPRESS FRESH FISH

J. Charles is a third generation specialist fish processing business in Aberdeen. It was founded some 70 years ago by Wilfred Charles on his return from the second world war. Wilfred earned great respect in the fish business for his attention to quality and ability to keep his demanding customers who were based in central London. His son

John, who had followed his father's interest in the food and drink industry joined the fish business on his return from tea planting in India. Continuing with the successful formula of never compromising with the quality the business continued to develop and flourish. John's son Andrew, who joined the family business some 35years ago has to this day continued the tradition of supplying their valued customers big or small with top quality service and product but also endeavoured to embrace the importance of using sustainable products.

MASTER CURERS & SMOKERS EST. 1857

John Ross jr is a traditional producer of luxury smoked salmon, using the traditional red brick kilns that have been in use since 1957. Scotland's largest exporter of traditionally smoked salmon, John Ross uses Grade A salmon, cold smoked over oak and beech chippings for up to 24 hours.

Another fish merchant Colin Fraser who has done very well for himself and lasted years with his top fish house and also top class filleters. Colin has been in business for over 30 years specialising in top quality skinless boneless counts. All his fish comes from sustainable fishing boats and is hand cut by his specialist filleters. They Java contracted 4 of the best fishing vessels in the fleet which allows them to guarantee their customers top quality all year round.

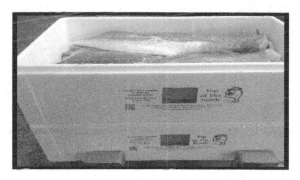

GAVIN McBAIN

STAFF AT COLIN FRASERS

COUPERS

Coupers seafoods is a family run business originally set up in 1987 by father and son team Daniel Couper jr and Daniel Couper senior, now also run by third generation Jamie Couper.

BILLY THOMSON
Danny was a woodside football player in his youth and one of the best fish merchants in his day

RONALD SCOTT
I started work at Derek Thomsons doing the pickle and smoking the haddock and also feeding the skinning machine, in my tea break I learned how to fin, then left to go to Coupers then Colin Frasers and then John Laws. In them days it was so easy to get a job in the fish.

JACQUELINE HUNTER
Maybe i'm a perfectionist, my brother Sonny Pearce had a fish house and my mum worked in the fish all her life, I remember going into the fish house at 8 or 9 years World. I learned to pack first, then learned to skin then fillet. I learned from the best.

DAVID DALGLEISH

I remember when Sonny Pearce, Sonny Fettes, and myself charted a small plane from Peter Cameron who owned Pegasus flying club to go down and see some customers, the plane was like a kite with wheels, some experience but good memories with the two Sonny's.

RUSSELL McLEOD

My father was manager at George Denny's who had a purpose built new place in the early mid seventies. I worked there every school holidays, then when I first left school. You had Gus the gaffer, Alan Marwick, Johnny Gray Dougie Skinner, Ally Anderson did all the smoking, Derek Mcqeen and my sister Sylvia, can't remember many of the girls because I was scared of them, they once threatened they were going to strip me in the box shed at tea time, didn't have tea break for a week, but great days indeed.

SHEILA HALLIGAN

I started off as a casual packer in Claben's with my mum packing yellow fish then onto pickles and tintering hanging the kippers, talk about sore thumbs and then finally became a filleter.

ARLEEN McDONALD

I used to be the roll wifie when I worked at Alec Ross, remember going down to the side door at low's the baker when I was nightshift. Worked in Trawlpac and remember waiting for our big fat xmas bonus only to be disappointed to get a fry of fish for xmas.

ELIZABETH GRAY

Started in the National with my mum at fifteen, then Pulfords with my oldest sister, back to the National as a filleter at sixteen, then the Coop, Jim Porters, Mcfisheries, Associated fisheries, casualling at Larry Fettes at nights, moved down to Coventry for eight years, then came home and back to the fish, Ross fish, Clabens, Starwood, Jatco, Trawlpac, Gramic and last job at Clipper. Mainly cut singles but cut flats and blocks as well. Fish trade was great for fitting in with kids hours at school, lots of good friends made along the way and many happy days.

RALMOND RICHARDS

Larry Little owned Starwood which was at the end of the chain bridge but was knocked down in the 70s, he then moved to a new factory at South Esplanade East, his partner was Harry Gun. He eventually went bust and the name changed to Runsborough, and Larry moved to Grimsby.

PERCY HUMPHREY

I worked with them all in Starwood, Dod Adams, Dod Herd, Crazy Dod Grey, Jim Wynes, Stan Robertson, Dave Clark, Brian Russell, Abby Smith, Brian Steal, Bobby Geddes young and old Tommy Ritchie and many more.

PATRICK McGUIRE

My first job in the fish was with GC Gove in the lane at the top of Comercial Quay around 1956, also in the lane was Ernest Gove who was the step father of Tory MP Michael Gove.

After Cable's lane that was us on the move again, we moved to the other side of the water in one of the lanes in Old Ford road, another shithole of a place! No hot water, mice everywhere but we liked it there. It only had room for a table of ten so we had to turn back a lot of work as we didn't have the staff or a chill to keep our fish in. The ten that was there was great guys and such a laugh. I remember working away at the table and having a debate with Dod Herd about who could run the fastest, because Dod and myself were well overweight guys, we both agreed on a £10 bet who could run round the lane the fastest, we go outside and back to back and when one of the guys said go we had to run around the lane and back again, Dod had to go one way and myself the other way. One of the boys shouted, "Go!" off Dod goes like the clappers as I just stood and watched him, we were all in stitches as they knew fine I wasn't going to run but it was worth paying the £10 just to see Dod coming round the corner out of breath and soaking of sweat. Good old Dod, what a character. Another day on a Sunday a few of us went in just to unload fish for us to cut on Monday morning, in comes one of the workers who had been on the piss all weekend, we was all having a laugh until he pulls out this gun to show us, we didn't think it was loaded then he starts shooting at the fish boxes, fuck me, we shit ourselves as it was loaded and the bullet went straight through the boxes.

We was settled in this place for months until my fish trade days came to an end. What we didn't realise was that for months the Social had hired an office across from us and was taking loads of pictures of us so they could get a good file on me and the staff.

I got a phone call from them one day asking me to come down to their main office. I walked in and there were about five of them around a table, I knew then that it was serious stuff. They came out with all the evidence that they had on me, pictures, times, the lot, but was shocked what they had to say, and tried to make a deal with me. Their deal was that if I told them the names of the merchants that was supplying me they would go after them as they was more interested in the big guys than me as they could hold them responsible for all the taxes, but if I didn't name them they would bill me for £25,000 which was a lot of money back then. I couldn't name the merchants as they had been so good to me over the years and just accepted the £25,000 tax bill.

THE TRAWLER MEN

In my view this brave men were the backbone and the heart of the fish trade, without them putting their lives at risk the fish trade would have been nothing. They say the Miners had the most dangerous and hardest jobs but without a doubt in my opinion it was the fishermen. Many lost their lives at sea, either during the war or treacherous weather. I used to love going down to the fish market to watch them unload their boats, and always said you would never get me on one of them even for a thousand pound a week.

British trawlers during the quarter – century after the end of world war two, when sailing smacks from the 1850s pushed further north in search of new grounds, they encountered colder and rougher weather. As a result they were away for much longer periods, with the average trip lasting about fourteen days. Unfortunately the vessels had the same crew facilities as traditional inshore vessels, which were away only overnight. This meant that the crew of a smack had cramped and poorly ventilated quarters heated only by small coal stoves. The cooking was done in the same area, which was lit simply by candles and oil lamps. There were no wash place or sanitary provision, and the bunks were simple planks of wood. Since the steam trawlers that came into service in the1890s had more space, conditions should have improved. But since their design allowed for a large fish hold and engine room, the only space available for crew accommodation was the foc'sle at the stem front, this was unsuitable because it was awkwardly shaped and separated from the rest of the vessel by the open deck. It was made more uncomfortable because in rough weather the bow would rise and fall alarmingly, forcing the men to wedge themselves in their bunks, especially the top ones, for fear of being thrown onto the steel floor as much as seven feet below. This area was also damp and cold because the added weight of the materials needed to fix this would have affected the vessel's stability and trim in bad weather. In 1935 Aberdeen distant water crews complained bitterly about the condition of the living quarters, which they described as primitive in the extreme, obsolescent and filthy. Twelve years later the crews in Aberdeen went on strike when things had not improved, neither proper medical provision nor adequate cleaning between trips and adequate food storage facilities.

The outcome was that even after eighteen hours on deck crews were not guaranteed a decent cooked meal, since the cook might well be incompetent or the food inedible, moreover the stores provided by the owners consisted of only basics bread, flour, jam, meat and potatoes, anything else had to be provided by the men themselves. Even as late as the 1960s crewmen had to provide their own "luxuries," such as tinned or fresh fruit. Many men brought oranges wrapped in tissue paper so that after consuming the fruit they could use the wrapping as toilet paper, as none was ever supplied as standard issue by the trawler owners. A further anomaly was that the skippers and mates received no food allowances, they either had to bring their own food or have its cost deducted from their shares at the end of the voyage.

The foc'sle started at the stem of the vessel to about 20ft aft, it was about 20ft in beam, this was the living quarters for sixteen men. There were no lockers for your gear, you simply kept three weeks change of clothing in your kit bag this you used mainly as a pillow. In the foc'sle would be an iron stove with an asbestos lagged flue running across the ceiling and out the aft end, this was the only means of heating and drying your wet gear, there would only be one or two light bulbs for illumination, no bunk lights, In this small space you kept your seaboots, guernseys, oilskins etc. the only ventilation was from the entrance to the deck, this was reached by a steep metal ladder which was very tricky to use in heavy weather. The food on board was very basic, flour , potatoes, fish, plus one joint of meat a day, if you had a good cook you could eat fairly well, but breakfast and tea was always fish. The other facilities were also inadequate, the mess room for example was not big enough for the entire crew to sit down for their meals. The amount and type of food supplied to the trawler crews was a serious problem, again it was the crews in Aberdeen who initially raised the issue, in april 1953 they demanded both a greater variety and quantity of food.

The food was put in the charge of the least qualified and lowest paid members of the crew, the cook who was usually an ex-trawlerman grown too old for deck work.

Training was simply making a few trips as an assistant to someone who had learned by the same method. The dangers of this method were apparent, since the cook had to provide meals for twenty men, three times a day for an average of twenty one days. The supplies would improve when the vessel reached the fishing grounds, for the cook could then have as much fish as he wanted. There were also constant problems over bread because only two days supply was put aboard when trawlers sailed, after this had been consumed it was up to the cook to bake the daily requirement a cook who could bake good bread and make a decent steam pudding was much appreciated and often followed a successful skipper from boat to boat. Such a skipper was only too aware that a well fed crew would work harder and cause less trouble. In 1967 three deckhands were fined a total of £32 with £18 costs, for refusing to work when mouldy flour prevented the baking of bread. The fact that until the mid 1960s no real training was given to cooks meant that crews had to suffer the consequences of incompetent and often slovenly cooks. The meat was put on top of the ice that filled up one of the fish holds on the way to the grounds, this had to be ventilated every other day as it was topped off with dry ice, then it was the job of the galley boy to retrieve some of the meat, then just before fishing commenced, the rest of the meat would be brought out and salted down for the homeward journey.

During the 1950s trawler owners were gradually forced to provide flush toilets and baths in their vessels, but only the minimum was done, for many of the newly fitted baths had no running water, which instead had to be pumped in and heated by means of a steam hose, in bad weather the water often froze, rendering the bath and toilet inoperable, the slightest bit of frost would put the toilet out of action. Then it was down to the stoke hold, on to a shoval cover with a bit of fine coal dust and into the furnace. If the chief was in a good mood, he would give you some cotton waste, otherwise it was newspaper or orange wrappings. The board of trade the ruled all boats had to have a toilet on board, the owners just cut a hole right through the boat put a hood over it and that was your toilet, it was very dangerous as you had to be there at the right time, when the ship was dipping its head you would get out like hell because when the ship came down a great spout of water shot out of the hole.

In 1959 new trawlers were to be built with crew accommodation in the aft section, other facilities were also improved as members of the B.T.F began for the first time to feel the effects of a labour shortage. The next configuration for accommodation specified cabins for the engineers, bosun and cook on the starboard side, and the skipper, mate and wireless officer. The deck crew were housed four to a cabin in four cabins in the stern, separate mess rooms were to be provided for officers and crew with adequate food storage space and refrigeration, heating was to be by a centralised system, which the more powerful diesal engines could provide. The provision of separate toilets, wash basins, baths and showers with hot and cold water, as well as adequate drying rooms for sea gear. The members of the crew usually took cards, dominoes, and books because there was nothing else for them to do.

The area which the UK lagged furthest behind its European contemporaries was in medical facilities, there were no legal requirement that any crew be trained in first aid, let alone that a vessel must carry a trained medical attendant or have a sick bay, despite the fact that the industry had the highest morbidity and mortality rates in Britain. The only legal requirement was a 1927 board of trade order requiring all vessels to carry medical stores and a copy of The Ship Captain's medical guide. During the 1960s helicopter rescue was available, but prevailing weather conditions often made this so hazardous that it was reserved only for those in extreme need. The lack of adequate medical facilities on British trawlers meant that their crews never received satisfactory medical help, a condition that in many cases could have been a factor in a crew members death. Vibration and constant noise not only helped make living conditions uncomfortable but also led to crew members making mistakes because they became disoriented.

The owners finally agreed to supply the men with bedding, what they eventually provided was one flock bed, one pillow and two blankets, but no sheets, these were only given to men who had filled out an application, back up by a fully up to date log book covering the previous three years and a medical certificate, the form had to be in twenty four hours before sailing, and the bedding had to be picked up from the local fishing vessel owners between 10.30am and 2.30 pm on the day of sailing. The meagreness was underlined by the fact thatonly one set of bedding was allowed per year, and it had tto be taken home to be cleaned.

The supply and use of alcohol on trawlers is a complex issue involving tradition, boredom, and sheer necessity. Men would often report back for duty at sailing time so inebriated that they were unfit for duty. The reasons for this however were not simply that trawlermen were heavy drinkers. Instead in many cases it had to do with acquiring enough courage to face another trip to sea. In line with naval tradition all trawlers carried a good supply of rum to act as a stimulant or a reward. They would look forward to their tot of rum in the morning or at the end of a stint on deck, it was put on board in two gallon jars by the company as part of the bond and was doled out by the skipper. Duty free liquor and tobacco was allowed to be carried if it left British waters. The bond was the sole responsibility of the skipper, who would sell tobacco as soon as the vessel was in international waters, but would only sell drink on the homeward voyage. The culture of ingrained drinking did not cause problems unless a member of the crew had a drinking problem, unfortunately due to the stress involved in trawling many men did especially during the 60s when the labour gap led to the hiring of men who might have been rejected in earlier years.

BILLY SHIRRAN

All trawlers that carried bond officially could not open there bond until they were past the 61st parallel. This being about 14-16 hour steam north of Shetland from Aberdeen. What did happen was when customs came down to check and lock up the bond locker, they left out a couple of bottles and a couple of cases of beer for the crew. When arriving back at Aberdeen the skipper would shout up to the roundhouse who would inform customs that a vessel with bond was docking. If customs were not at the vessel when all moored up it was a mad scramble to get ashore and out of the area before they did arrive, NOT saying I did this lol.

ANDREW MORTIMER

My da and I think all trawlermen wouldn't sail without their bottle of rum, that they were unofficially allowed, my da had his bottle every sail day. Each man got two bottles of beer per day from the bond, they would save them up and get pissed once a week.

By 1950s after years of inter war neglect the fishing industry was handicapped by a run down and out of date fleet of vessels, a large proportion of which were still coal burning. Out of 197 ships operating from Aberdeen 172 had been built before 1929 and of these 154 had been built before 1919. There were middle distance trawlers, smaller classes which would fish relatively close to the north east and west coast of Scotland. In addition to steam and diesel powered side trawlers there was the larger purpose built line boats Mac would fish up to 28 days in depths down to 400 fathoms targeting halibut.

During the late 70s and early 80s a number of seine net vessels were built such as the Starwood, Annwood, don wood. During the 1990s and early 2000s the fishing industry started to decline as stocks decreased and restrictive external legislation was introduced, many vessels were decommissioned and those that survived faced hardships for a number of years until key stocks started to improve. The waters formerly fished by British fishermen were now being fished by German trawlers. A regular invasion of Germen trawlers challenged the fishing industry of Aberdeen, but this menace was removed by by British trawl-owners and skippers having prevailed on the auctioneers not to sell fish landed by German vessels fishing in the north sea. The British fishermen went on strike until the landing of fish from German trawlers was stopped. The skipper of a German trawler who proposed to discharge his large catch of fish was told to take his fish to Germany. This decision did not affect German catches made in Icelandic waters.

Some 3000 trawlermen and sympathisers went on strike for about a month and a near riot took place when ice and fish were thrown at the German crewmen and one German trawler's catch was dumped in the Albert basin. Market porters were beaten up for moving the fish and there were police baton charges after suitable reinforcements arrived.

THE TRAGEDIES

The trawler "**Blue Crusader**" left Aberdeen on the 13th of January 1965 with a crew of thirteen, she was in radio contact with another trawler at 7.30 pm that evening near Orkney, there was a force 10 gale that night, as soon as it was reported that the trawler was overdue, all shipping was alerted and an extensive air search lasting three days over the whole of Orkney and Shetland area. Among those on board was 15 year old Colin Kay, the tragedy left 11 widows and 28 children fatherless.

On November 1994, the Hartepool trawler "**Doris Burton**" which was built at Hall Russells left Aberdeen and vanished. Three weeks she had been based at Aberdeen short tripping spending two or three days at sea fishing and then landing her catch at the fish market.

Ben Doran was built by ship builders Hall Russell and it was launched on 3rd march 1900 and operated until its wrecking in Shetland on 29th march 1930, which claimed the lives of the full crew, believed to number nine crew members. Its wrecking has been called the most tragic wreck in Shetland's history.

TRAWLER ALMOST SWAMPED.

Aberdeen Vessel in Teeth of Gale.

SWEPT BY GIGANTIC WAVES.

Crew safe as N.E. boat sinks

THREW PARAFFIN IN FURNACE.

Trawler Fireman Injured By Explosion.

Still no answer from Loch Brora

THERE IS still no answer to the mystery silence surrounding the Aberdeen line-ishing boat Loch Brora, which has not made radio contact with shore for nearly a week.

STRUCK BY BOARD.

Mate of Aberdeen Trawler Dies at Sea.

ABERDEEN TRAWLER CREW'S LEAP TO SAFETY.

Vessel Sinks After Collision With Steamer.

ENORMOUS HOLE TORN IN SIDE.

DRAMA OF IMPENETRABLE NORTH SEA FOG.

FISHERMAN DIES OF INJURIES

SCALDED BY WATER FROM LIVER BOILER

BROTHERS DROWNED.

Washed Overboard from Trawler.

These are clips from our local newspapers which would be on a regular basis.

Aberdeen Trawler Crew All Safe.

UNCERTAIN FATE OF TWO RESCUERS.

A search for ten of the crew of the trawler "Robert Limbreck" which sank in a gale off the Scottish coast was abandoned as it feared that the crew had not survived. The bodies of two men believed to be members of the crew and a dinghy were washed ashore on the northern shore off the Island of Mull.

The **Strathalian** 1972 a victim of a spring tide in the fish-market harbour. The trawler was trapped under the quay during a rising tide, she sank and took an adjacent trawler the **George Wood** with her, both vessels were raised and the Strathalian was sold for scrap and the George Wood returned to fishing.

TERRY ALI
Another tragedy was two boats entering the harbour in storm conditions were both bashed against the rocks at the mouth of the harbour.

Only one seaman escaped from the gale-ravaged Aberdeen trawler the **George Robb** early yesterday morning and he died from exposure under the Duncansby head cliffs near John o' Groats as rescue teams searched for the wreck. He was found at first light wearing only a shirt and life jacket crouched against the death dealing hurricane among the shingle near high water mark, behind him his 11 shipmates perished in the trawler, not 50 yards from the shore and safety. A tiny cove, cut deep into the 200ft high cliffs, was the only shelter from the storm that ripped the bottom from the 29 year-old boat as it sailed for Faroe fishing grounds. The man dark haired and aged about 30 was within yards of the cleft in the high sea wall, he was found by two John o' Groat's men making an early morning search for survivors as the slackening gale screamed and tore at their clothes. They were almost certain the man was alive when he reached the shore in darkness, he did not look as he had been washed up, he must have died as he crouched down in the slack water trying to ward off the wind. Fishermen in Aberdeen were surprised that the George Robb had made the Pentland Firth in such quick time, but the gale that hounded her at times gusted at more than 80 miles an hour. The boat was recently converted at a cost of £45,000 from coal to diesel. It sailed at 11.30 on Sunday morning for a 14 day fishing trip to the Faroes.

The owners of the boat said "that two of the men who sailed were "liners" men who work the fishing boats, and had just joined the George Robb to get extra money for Christmas".

On board was 30 year old James Findlay of Davidson place, this was the third time he had been involved in a sea accident. He was aboard the Sturdee when it went aground on the Aberdeen beach, and also on the George Robb when it grounded in Orkney. He and his wife were to have celebrated a wedding anniversary the next day.

A third member of the crew 45 year old Albert Smith, father of four and had a mate's ticket, but had been out of work for three weeks, he took this job as a deck hand just to get money for Christmas.

It was the same story in all the homes where hopes for a merry Xmas had been dashed on the foam covered rocks of Duncansby Head for this family tragedy. A tragedy for the Robbs one of the most closely knit family trawling concerns in the port and a tragedy for the families of the men who sailed on the George Robb.

Nancy Dugan the wife of second engineer, summed it up when she said "Bob was so pleased about the new boat. He even invited me down to see it, Bob who would have been 39 was coming home for Christmas to his wife and two sons aged 5 and 9 and his daughter aged 7. Nancy said "he was anxious to get the house painted before he left and had been working hard to have it ready for Xmas and the new year. Nancy was getting her little girl ready for school when she heard about the boat on the radio.

William Mackay the 35 year old chief engineer, hated the sea and spent every minute in port at his home in Strathmore drive, he was a father of three children aged from 13 months to seven years. His last words to his wife as he left home were "maybe I'll be back as it looks gey rough" his wife said "he had been hoping for a shore job so that he wouldn't have to go to sea.

Mr Campbell had raced to the spot after receiving the trawlers position, his squad of 30 men joined by life savers from Scarfskerry carried heavy rescue gear almost a mile across treacherous bogland to the cliff. Marshall Ryles the 31 year old skipper fought a losing battle with the killer gale, the bold skipper a dashing father of four called his wife by radio-phone at her home in North Anderson drive four hours before the ship foundered on the rocks. His last words was i'm in for a rough night, the weathers bad.

KATE McGREGOR

My dad and uncles were on a boat that sank, they were in a lifeboat for days, it was going to Germany to be scrapped, they had given up, apart from my uncle Charlie who ate tobacco to keep him awake, this was in the sixties, we stayed in the Castlegate at the time, first I knew was when the reporters came to my door.

GEORGE WOOD

I was on the Avon river, Bill Clark was the skipper we were coming home from Iceland, running before a north west force 12, I was on watch and it was that bad the skipper stayed in the wheel house, that's how bad it was as they never did that. We took a wave and the boat shuddered, then she took a second wave and luckily we missed the third wave, the skipper put her full speed ahead and she cleard the deck and he got her around as we was going head into it. We slowed down the speed, and what a difference and just kept it like that until daylight, then turned around and set course back home to Aberdeen. I was on the wheel at the time and said to myself this is it, but the good lord was looking after us. What really got to me was it was only 6 weeks before that I got rescued by the lifeboat when we ran ashore on the West of Orkney on the Strathcoe. I went through a lot of bad mishaps in my days as a trawlerman. The people in Aberdeen did not know the truth about they way we were treated and the conditions we had to put up with, the trawlers were so rusted they would just give them a paint job, they would not chip away the rust because it would go right through the boat, there were more rats than you could count, and that is why we drank to live and lived to drink.

GEORGE WOOD

TWO H.M. TRAWLERS SUNK AFTER BOMBING

H.M. TRAWLER FORT ROYAL, which was registered at Aberdeen

LOWESTOFT
She was a 163 grt steam trawler that was sunk on 11th march 1941 by aircraft bombing and gunfire.

ACTIVE
She was a 185 grt steam trawler that was sunk on 18th December 1939 by a torpedo fired by an aircraft at a position 48 miles north west of Ratray Head.

ARORA
She left Aberdeen on 23rd January 1941 but was never seen again, they found her lifeboat on the West Coast of Orkney riddled with bullets and containing bomb splinters.

BASS ROCK
She was a 169 grt steam trawler that was sunk on 24th September 1940 by an aircraft bombing off the head of kinsale.

ST GEORGE
Attacked and sunk by submarine gunfire, all the crew were taken prisoners. 2nd may 1915.

MARTABAN
Captured by submarine, sunk by gunfire. 2nd may 1915.

CRUISER
Attacked and sunk by submarine gunfire, 4 lives lost including the skipper.

SUNRAY
Captured by submarine, sunk by gunfire.

MERCURY
Captured by submarine, sunk by gunfire.

GAZEHOUND
Captured by submarine, sunk by gunfire.

CURLEW
Captured by submarine, sunk by gunfire.

R.I.P
TO ALL THE BRAVE MEN WHO LOST THEIR LIVES
AT SEA

BOB CUSITER

I feel my story of my brother in law who is no longer with us might amuse some folks, you see he was part of the first recorded mutiny on a fishing boat out of Aberdeen. Billy Massie and a few others thought it would be a good idea to play mary graig and head to sea, I have no doubt alcohol played a big part in this, however the pirates didn't get that far really, so when the booze dried up there wasn't a lot more to do but head for the nearest port. His time in Craiginches Prison for that was not wasted as his job was to make fish nets.

GEORGE DOUGLAS ROSS

My old man went trawling and I remember that nearly every trawlerman had a folding wooden handle knife in their possession which my old man said was his filleting knife.

JAMES PAUL

They were gutting, mending, filleting and tattie peeling knives, Nest, Venture, Lowen, Messer were the ones they used.

JIM THORBURN

My dad and uncles used the venturer knife, you often seen them stuck under their caps, another thing they all used to have was the faroe lighters.

DOUG GOVE

I don't have a seagoing tale to tell other than to say when I was about ten I did two trips, first with my uncle George

Bruce, not sure if he was skipper or mate as he did both, second was with my dad who hailed from Portnockie and went deckie all his days. Although only a wee boy I took a turn at gutting and helping on watch as well as helping in the galley. Looking back what a wonderful experience for me and of course completely out of order when compared to today's standards. I remember the sea breaking over the wheelhouse but also beautiful calm weather, there is no doubt it was the stink on board that made me sick on both trips, I got ten bob as wages for each trip. One of the more unsavoury aspects of trawling in those days was taking care of nature, I went three days without 'going' but had to give in and sat in the deck focastie toilet looking up into the wheelhouse, yes, you had to use newspaper, everybody else just 'went' over the side.

GEORGE WOOD

In my days there was a lot of superstition on board the boats, some things you would not say or do. It was unlucky to do or say "no woman on board" you did not say the word "salmon" you just called it red fish, you did not kill a rat, and would not leave a sinking ship, and most of all was you did not whistle as the skipper would shout at you and say "there is enough fucking wind without you adding to it. Oslo a north region skipper would not sail on a Sunday, one good thing about that was we still got our day's pay, so we got an extra day in to get drunk, those were the days I will never forget.

A very good friend of mine June (Poona) Smith had a big article about her in the local newspaper back in the early seventies. She was one of the first female ever to go trawling.

GEORGE AND POONA BAXTER

Home from the fishing grounds of Iceland, where she gutted fish on the deck is 14 year old Aberdeen school girl June Baxter. She spent her Easter holidays stowing fish in the trawlers fish room, helping the cook to make rowies and being on watch with the officers as the ship ploughed through mountaines seas. June is the daughter of skipper George Baxter who commands the crack trawler Ben Brackie, and she dearly wants to follow in his footsteps.

June has just returned from a 17 day trip on board the Ben Brackie, the only bad weather she encountered was coming through the Pentland firth on the passage home. At her aunts home at 21 Bremner terrace where she stays, she said that she would go back to the isolated world of the fishermen tomorrow if I could, the prospect of a onshore job when she leaves school did not appeal to her, I would like to go back to sea, not on a large ship as a stewardess or a radio operator, but as a deck hand, she said earnestly. The formalities of "signing on" June as a supernumary were observed before she sailed with the Ben Brackie, which took three and a half days to reach the fishing grounds of Icelands west coast.

GEORGE WOOD

People of today wouldn't understand what we went through. I paid into the shipwreck manors the penny a day to the trawlermans pension and never got a penny back. They called us drunken bums if we refused to sail, they would call the police who would take us up to lodge walk to spend the night in the cells, next day we went before Judge Hamilton who hated trawlermen, we was found guilty, five pounds fine or 28 days in jail. If we didn't have the money we went straight to jail, two or three days later a runner would come and see you and said they needed a deck hand or a fireman for their boat, if you said yes they would pay your fine. You was released and signed on to the boat, got a day's pay then went and got drunk then sailed the next day, when you got home the first thing they took of your money was the five pound fine, which was a weeks pay also took of your food and bond money, which left you with peanuts.

ADELE RANKINE

I remember the power strikes in the early seventies, I worked in Stillies at the time when we tried to get our orders out before the power went off, this was in the winter time, no health and safety in them days, I remember we had to get this order out but we had no lights, John Still told our driver to keep the lights on in his lorry so we could get the order out, no hot water for dips you just had to carry on, it was the same when the pipes froze in the winter, if you went for your teabreak when you got back your knife was frozen to the board. But we all just had to get on with it.

KAREN HUNTER

It was hard work in the fish trade, my brother had his own table in the Arches, I never touched a fish up until then and I was only 14 years old I was not very good as they never asked me back again, then after I had my kids I went to work for Polar fish at night, I told the boss I had experience so when he asked me to get my fish clobber from the store and when I was ready had to meet him at the tunnel, flpping heck I was looking everywhere for a tunnel to walk through, but he was talking about the tunnel freezer machines. Then went to work for Freddy Paterson on day shift, brilliant laughs great bunch of ladies I worked with, but couldn't get round the fish twang when speaking. Stopped work to have my son and then went back working at Trawlpack on the night shift and that was a great job and great laughs we had, but couldn't do that job now as it would kill me.

EDWARD FLETCHER

George hendry I think it was in number 2 arch, George used to ask me to but a box of lemon sole's, he would say just buy that box! In 1983 a large box of lemons was about £120 a box, buyers would run me up to £160 that was expensive then, but stupid prices now, the trade has gone out of control and soon there will be no fish merchants. I had great memories of the Aberdeen market, it was good times everyone working together.

COLIN EVANS

You know something we all worked in the fish, that is where we were born to be in. I look back on my time in the fish trade, Saturday mornings with Jim Edmonds pulling fish from Peterhead harbour.

WILLIAM RIDDOCH

Brings it all back fab times and a lot of good people. Salt of the earth.

CHRISTINE FRASER

I remember standing in pans of hot water and how sore the chill blanes were, it was the good old days but I loved it and I love the smell of fish today, brings back happy memories.

HILDA THOMPSON

Those were the good days, hard work, plenty money to be made if you were willing to work for it, always lots of laughing and singing as we worked. Great people and loved the fish trade.

JUDI MARTIN
My late father was a detective, and knew almost all the fish merchants due to frequent break -ins and having grown up and policed in Torry. He came home frequently with a parcel of fish.

CATHERINE JOHNSTON
I started in Jatco seafood, worked the breading machine then the freezer tunnel, then Jim Mckerron learnt me to fillet, then moved to Coopers, then on to Direct fish where Dick Gribble was my boss. My last job was in Andy Ewans for a few years. I miss the laughs and the fights it was the best job ever.

JAMES FARQUHAR
Great times in my last job cutting big coley at Duguids in Tullos with Sugar, Johnny Gray, and Wattie Stevens, great days and off to the Portland club when we finished work.

LYN WOOD
Remember sitting at the river side in my lunch breaks with my wellies on eating my sandwiches, also no one sat next to you on the bus home because of the smell.

MANDY ROBERSTSON
My late dad was a trawlerman Billy Robertson also we'll known as briggies, my late mum Nessie Robertson worked in the fish all of her life too, she worked in many a fish houses.. Tommy Wilson's.. Alfie Nicol and many more. I also worked in the fish and had a saturday job at Alfie Nicols and worked there after I left school. Good times.

LESLEY MILNE

My dad was a trawlerman his name was Richard Whyte, he moved office all the time, my step father Alex Main was on the Ben Gulvain, George Baxter was there skipper, my father in law was on the Fairtry but I think it sailed out of Grimsby. They are all gone now, only my step uncle Michael Main is still with us. In memory to them all I have made the Fisherman's Mission my charity of choice.

GEORGE WOOD

I was a long time with the Ben boats, Charlie Chase was the runner, also on the Ben Leo with Harry Bowman and the only time we made good money. I got my 2nd fish ticket and then went for my mates ticket, but no good after I got ship wrecked on the Strathcoe and lost my pal Dave Falconer overboard on the Souvenir. I moved to Canada and came back to chat to all my fishermens kids as all of my friends have gone now. I had 4 brothers who all went trawling who are no longer with us. I would like to come home to Aberdeen one more time before I kick the bucket.

Had to end the book with the last words from this remarkable man George Wood. I loved hearing all his stories. This book was set out for all the people that never worked in our brilliant trade, also to bring back great memories. Would be true to say that there will never be an industry like what we all witnessed ever again. Most of the people that worked in the fish industry said it was the best job they ever worked in.

Made in the USA
Coppell, TX
03 November 2020